Who's Afraid of the
JUDGMENT?

Roy Gane

The good news about Christ's work in the heavenly sanctuary

Pacific Press® Publishing Association
Nampa, Idaho
Oshawa, Ontario, Canada
www.pacificpress.com

Book design by Dennis Ferree
Cover illustration © Justinen Creative Group

Unless otherwise marked, Scripture quotations are from the NASB, the *New American Standard Bible,* © The Lockman Foundation 1960, 1962, 1963, 1968, 1971, 1972, 1973, 1975, 1977. Used by permission.

Scripture quotations marked (NRSV) are taken from the New Revised Standard Version of the Bible, copyright © 1989 by the Division of Christian Education of the National Council of the Churches of Christ in the USA. Used by permission. All rights reserved.

Scripture quotations marked (NKJV) are taken from the *Holy Bible,* New King James Version, copyright © 1979, 1980, 1982 by Thomas Nelson, Inc. Used by permission.

Scripture quotations marked (The New JPS) are taken from the *Tanakh: The Holy Scriptures, The New JPS Translation According to the Traditional Hebrew Text.* Copyright © 1985, The Jewish Publication Society. Used by permission.

Scripture quotations marked (NAU) are taken from the New American Standard Bible Update.

Scripture quotations marked (NIV) are taken from the *Holy Bible, New International Version,* copyright © 1973, 1978, 1984 by the International Bible Society. Used by permission of Zondervan Bible Publishers.

Library of Congress Cataloging-in-Publication Data

ISBN: 0-8163-2128-0
ISBN 13: 9780816321285

Additional copies of this book are available by calling toll free 1-800-765-6955 or by visiting <http://www.adventistbookcenter.com>.

06 07 08 09 10 • 5 4 3 2 1

Table of Contents

Introduction: Overview of Good News About the Judgment

This book, *Who's Afraid of the Judgment?* is intended to be a simple introduction to the profound and timely Bible teaching that God demonstrates His character of love through a judgment in His heavenly sanctuary before Christ's second coming.[1]

Most Christians have missed the fact that such a judgment exists. And many of those who recognize the fact of the judgment and its timing have misunderstood its purpose, so the event fills them with terror and undermines their assurance of salvation in Christ. But the biblical book of Daniel, drawing on profound concepts of atonement in Leviticus and paving the way for further understanding in the New Testament books of Hebrews and Revelation, shows us that the pre-Advent judgment *benefits* God's loyal people. Daniel 7:22 says "judgment was given *for* the holy ones of the Most High" (NRSV, emphasis supplied).

Within the context of the great war (or "great controversy") between good and evil in which we find ourselves, God calls broken, fallen human beings to restoration through the sacrifice of His Son. By dying the ultimate death of separation from God (Matthew 27:46; compare Revelation 20) for the entire human race, Jesus has accomplished several crucial things.

1. He has reclaimed His clear title to dominion over this world (see Daniel 7:13, 14, which pictures Him gaining dominion because of His role as "Son of Man"; see also Revelation 5).

2. Therefore, He can restore to saved human beings the dominion that He delegated to Adam, Eve, and their descendants at Creation (Genesis 1:28), which Satan usurped (John 12:31) by deceiving our first parents regarding the character of God (Genesis 3).

3. He has died the death that is "the wages of sin" in order to give us "the free gift" of "eternal life" (Romans 6:23, NRSV). This gift is a breathtakingly comprehensive package. It includes forgiveness for our acts of un-love (in other words, *sin;* see 1 John 1:9), reclaiming us from our lives of sinning by the renewal/rebirth of our spiritual minds through the presence of Christ brought by the Holy Spirit (John 3:5–8; Romans 5:5; Galatians 2:20; Titus 3:4–7) and the transformation of our mortal bodies at Christ's second coming (1 Corinthians 15:51–54).

4. Christ's sacrifice makes it possible for God to extend mercy to those who believe without compromising His justice (Romans 3:26), the other side of His character of love. And through the gospel, God heals His universe from dangerous doubt regarding His character by proving His perfect love.

If God were defective either in justice or in mercy, He would not be the God of perfect love that He claims to be (1 John 4:8). And if it were not true that God is love in the ultimate sense, He couldn't expect His created beings to live by love. Consequently, He couldn't hold His universe together, because the ones He has created would be affected and infected by un-love, which would cause them eventually to destroy each other. It is because of the crucial importance of love that "the wages of sin is death" (Romans 6:23, NRSV). Only those who live by the moral principle of love can continue to live in God's universe.

Christ's once-for-all atoning death on the cross (Hebrews 9:28) completed the foundational event of salvation history (John 19:30, " 'It is finished' " [NRSV].) from which all reconciliation with God flows. It is only because of Christ's sacrifice that we can have freedom from condemnation and peace with God (Romans 5:1; 8:1). Christ's sacrifice is so great that reconciliation/atonement ("at-one-ment") continues to flow unabated from Calvary almost two thousand years later, as the Lamb carries the Cross event with Him to keep its benefits ever fresh (Revelation 5:6).

However, Christ's death alone could not give us eternal life. Having died for our sins, He must rise from the grave to conquer the death that results from sin (1 Corinthians 15:12–26). Because He now lives, He is ministering as High Priest in God's heavenly temple in order to distribute the purifying power of His sacrifice to each of us every day as we need it (Hebrews 9:11–14). Without this, salvation would be available, but it would not benefit us. It would be like a grant of ten million dollars for a scholarship fund that helps nobody because it stays in the bank, never reaching the needy students for which it was intended.

Even beyond Christ's resurrection and high-priestly ministry in heaven, Revelation 14 tells us that the gospel, bought by Christ's sacrifice, continues into the end time, just before Christ comes to earth again: "I saw another angel flying in midheaven, having *an eternal gospel* to preach to those who live on the earth, and to every nation and tribe and tongue and people; and he said with a loud voice, 'Fear God, and give Him glory, because *the hour of His judgment has come;* and worship Him who made the heaven and the earth and sea and springs of waters' " (verses 6, 7; emphasis supplied).

Notice that the "angel" has "an eternal gospel" for the whole world and that this proclamation of the gospel calls everyone to honor and worship God as Creator "because the hour of His judgment *has come.*" Here is a judgment before Christ's second coming—that is, a pre-Advent judgment that has a beginning point in the end time and calls people to show loyalty to Christ. This is the same end-time judgment as that prophesied in Daniel 7, which is for the benefit of God's oppressed holy people, who welcome judgment on their behalf, just as the psalmist cried out, "Arise, O God, judge the earth" (Psalm 82:8). The judgment is good news![2]

Judgment is the fulfillment of humanity's hopes and yearnings. In our minds, it conveys the ideas of crime and punishment and inspires fear and apprehension. The Bible, however, sees judgment from the viewpoint of the oppressed, the suffering victim, and thus places it in the context of salvation and victory over the oppressor and evil. Israelite culture already recognized that fact on a national level. The judges of Israel were war heroes who would crush the enemy. Scripture also referred to them as saviors (Judges 3:9, 15; 6:36; 12:3). This two-level

6

aspect of the judgment of God is especially clear in the psalms that describe the judging God as both savior and avenger (Psalms 18:47, 48; 58:11; 94:1–6, 22, 23; 149:4, 7, 9; etc.). Such a depiction of God can shock our modern sensibilities. And yet just coaxing the lion into letting go of the lamb will not work. To save the lamb, one must overcome the lion. That is why the term *tsedaqa,* which means "justice," implying the punishment of the oppressor, also means "love," as it liberates the oppressed back to life.[3]

The pre-Advent judgment is the subject of the present book. Why does God need this judgment? On what are the results of this judgment based? When does the judgment begin? How do we participate and show loyalty to God?

We will find that the purpose of the judgment is to demonstrate before the universe of God's created beings that He is just and fair because He has justified the right people—namely, those who believe (Romans 3:26)—on the basis of Christ's sacrifice. The foundation for this justifying of God was fully established at the Cross, but it was not yet clear who would receive the gift of faith in Jesus—that is, living faith that works through love (Galatians 5:6; James 2:26). The judgment is about who has received grace through faith (Ephesians 2:8, 9) as demonstrated in the life empowered by God and His Holy Spirit after conversion. It is not about who has sinned, because everyone knows that all human beings have done that (Romans 3:23).

We will learn when the pre-Advent judgment began and why this is so important for modern Christians to understand. The timing of the beginning of the judgment is not a stand-alone doctrine. It is significant because God has revealed when we need to coordinate our loyal devotion to Him with the final stage of His grand atonement process as loyal Israelites were to do in a smaller sense on the awesome Day of Atonement (see Revelation 14:12; Leviticus 16:29–31; 23:26–32). And because key aspects of the pre-Advent judgment—especially its timing—have been under attack, we will answer some objections in order to show how solid this biblical teaching is.

This book is limited in purpose and scope. For more information on the pre-Advent judgment, Daniel, the gospel, and related topics, the reader is directed to other resources, a number of which are cited in the endnotes. Such books include Ellen G. White's *The Great Controversy; The Seventh-day Adventist Bible Commentary* series; the

WHO'S AFRAID OF THE JUDGMENT?

Daniel and Revelation Committee Series volumes edited by Frank Holbrook (especially volumes 1–3); William Shea's *Daniel;* Jacques Doukhan's *Secrets of Daniel;* Gerhard Pfandl's *Daniel: The Seer of Babylon;* Mervyn Maxwell's *God Cares;* Brempong Owusu-Antwi's *The Chronology of Daniel 9:24-27;* Alberto Treiyer's *The Day of Atonement and the Heavenly Judgment;* John Anderson's *Investigating the Judgment;* Clifford Goldstein's *1844 Made Simple;* Erwin Gane's *Jesus Only;* and my *Altar Call* and *Leviticus, Numbers* commentary, to name a few.

Note carefully: Just because I cite an author as helpful regarding a certain point does not mean that I agree with everything that that author writes, teaches, or preaches. Like the Bereans, we need to evaluate every statement of every human (and therefore fallible) communicator in light of Scripture on a case-by-case basis, rather than doing "knee-jerk" reactions based on prejudice or simplistic "litmus tests."

Because Scripture is the authoritative source for our understanding of all aspects of salvation, I quote many Bible passages. And because the New American Standard Bible attempts to be quite literal and precise and stays close to the original, I have used it as my default translation, referring to others by abbreviations (NKJV, NRSV, The New JPS, etc.). However, I derive my conclusions from the original Hebrew, Aramaic, and Greek texts that constitute the Bible.

---

1. For the idea that love is justice, see Jacques Doukhan, *Daniel: The Vision of the End,* revised ed. (Berrien Springs, Mich.: Andrews University Press, 1987), 41.

2. Richard M. Davidson, "The Good News of Yom Kippur," *Journal of the Adventist Theological Society* 2 (1996): 4–27. Davidson points out three major reasons why the end-time Day of Atonement judgment is good news: "(1) It restores the gospel to its rightful place, bringing to the believer assurance and vindication in the judgment; (2) it accomplishes the cleansing of the heavenly sanctuary and its earthly counterpart, the soul temples of the saints; and (3) it vindicates the character of God" (23).

3. Jacques Doukhan, *Secrets of Daniel: Wisdom and Dreams of a Jewish Prince in Exile* (Hagerstown, Md.: Review and Herald, 2000), 112, 113.

8

The Great War Over God's Character

People do not usually choose to place themselves in dire straits. These situations come uninvited. Many disasters—such as tsunamis, earthquakes, and terrorist attacks—strike quickly and with brutal and devastating force. Others—such as famines, epidemics (AIDS, for instance), and wars—can last for weeks or even for generations. England and France once fought a series of conflicts known collectively as the Hundred Years' War (1337–1453). Even now, some people live their entire lives in war zones.

Correction: *All* people, including you and I, have lived their entire lives in a war zone. This war isn't a regional conflict over who rules a few hundred square miles. It isn't merely a civil war or an ethnic cleansing, as devastating as those can be. It isn't even a "World War," the last of which embroiled nations from most of the continents and claimed the lives of more than forty million people. It is far bigger than that. No human being on any body of land or sea has ever been able to escape the clutches of this great war. It has killed billions of human beings and nobody knows how many trillions of other creatures. In fact, only two people have ever escaped death in this war: Enoch (Genesis 5:24) and Elijah (2 Kings 2:11).

The great war isn't even limited to planet Earth! Jesus Christ Himself, the Son of God, fell as a casualty in the conflict. He told

Pilate that His kingdom is not based in this world (John 18:36); He rules a far wider domain. So, the war is not only here, and it is not only about us, even though we are caught in the middle of it.

When you've lived your entire life in a war zone, emergencies seem normal. You don't know anything different. Consequently, many people simply accept suffering, pain, sorrow, and death as inevitable—the way things are supposed to be. The ancient Egyptians glorified and immortalized death as a passage to continuation of life in another form. Death was good and holy. Every tomb was a temple. Countless other groups have also been in a state of denial, not understanding or admitting that we are afflicted by a great war. Weren't good and evil, such as the Oriental yin and yang, part of the "plan" from the beginning? Isn't death an original, integral, and necessary part of life, which goes in cycles of reincarnation? Or would that mean "reincarceration"—imprisonment all over again in the deadly grip of mortality?

A modern person who is attempting to live an ideal life—and succeeding quite well at it—may not need an Eastern philosophy to put the idea of a great war far away. Life is secure, comfortable, and pleasant much of the time. Everything is under control. Hardly any problem arises that one's work associates, physician, stockbroker, insurance agent, or government can't fix. But then a car accident, a serious illness, a divorce, or a death in the family intrudes on the "good life" and brings home the haunting reality that something is drastically wrong.

Are we being melancholy, morbid, and paranoid if we reflect on our dilemma? After all, life holds a lot of joy; there is so much for which we can be thankful. There are sunsets, dear family members and friends, health, good food, trees, flowers, music, and pets. Even in the midst of war, there are islands of peace. So, we encounter radical contrast and tension between two basic categories of experience: the good and the bad, the painful and the pleasurable.

Origin of the great war

Where did the great war and the two kinds of experience come from? This is not merely a historical question—the conflicts we encounter shape our lives and attitudes. It is the sources of these conflicts that largely determine their nature. On a smaller scale, the outlook and lives of an entire generation of people were forged on the anvil of World War II, which arose from the dark ambitions of European fascists and Asian warlords and the (fortunately success-ful) attempt of other powers to stop them.[1] So, who started the great war? The Bible tells us.

Originally, all was peace and perfection. The hand of God, the Creator, made everything good. Then something happened—a paradox in Paradise. God told the story later, giving the culprit the literary title "king of Tyre":

" ' "You were in Eden, the garden of God. . . .
You were the anointed cherub who covers,
And I placed you there.
You were on the holy mountain of God;
You walked in the midst of the stones of fire.
You were blameless in your ways
From the day you were created,
Until unrighteousness was found in you.
By the abundance of your trade
You were internally filled with violence,
And you sinned;
Therefore I have cast you as profane
From the mountain of God.
And I have destroyed you, O covering cherub,
From the midst of the stones of fire.
Your heart was lifted up because of your beauty;
You corrupted your wisdom by reason of your splendor.
I cast you to the ground;
I put you before kings,
That they may see you" ' " (Ezekiel 28:13–17).

So the problem started with none other than a mighty angel—"the anointed cherub who covers," who was closer to God than any-one else was! He became proud because of his beauty. But he didn't just look at himself and ask rhetorically, "Mirror, mirror on the wall, who's the fairest one of all?" Through the prophet Isaiah, God tells us more. This time He addresses the originator of evil as the "king of Babylon":

" 'How you have fallen from heaven,
O star of the morning, son of the dawn!
You have been cut down to the earth,
You who have weakened the nations!
But you said in your heart,
"I will ascend to heaven;
I will raise my throne above the stars of God,
And I will sit on the mount of assembly
In the recesses of the north.
I will ascend above the heights of the clouds;
I will make myself like the Most High" ' " (Isaiah 14:12–14).

Here is the stuff of which wars are made: The servant presumed to dethrone his master, as many servants have done in subsequent human history. But in this case it was the Master of the entire universe, so the stakes were high and the war would be a great one. Indeed, it has been great, as John saw: "There was war in heaven, Michael and his angels waging war with the dragon. And the dragon and his angels waged war, and they were not strong enough, and there was no longer a place found for them in heaven. And the great dragon was thrown down, the serpent of old who is called the devil and Satan, who deceives the whole world; he was thrown down to the earth, and his angels were thrown down with him" (Revelation 12:7–9).

Originator of the great war

So the fallen angel was the one we now call "the devil" or "Satan" (literally, the *satan*, "the adversary"). He is the leader of a group of angels, now called "demons," whom he led in rebellion against God.

For many people these days, the devil or Satan is merely a cultural artifact like Santa Claus. In America at Halloween, some people wear humorously garish devil costumes. Satan has become a subject of comedy. Flip Wilson provoked barrels of laughs when he said, "The devil made me do it!" Jokes and cartoons depict the devil as the horned, pitchfork-wielding overseer of hell who is on our side in the sense that he enjoys tormenting our enemies in all kinds of delightfully frightful ways.

But even twisted modern entertainment holds hints that the devil is not on our side. When you see a picture of Marilyn Manson, a male rock star who is a sinister minister of the church of Satan and rather convincingly impersonates his diabolical master, you get the impression that behind the occult-friendly gloss of Disney and Harry Potter magic there is a darker reality. You wonder if it is coincidence that Manson was a favorite of Eric Harris and Dylan Klebold, the teenage boys who carried out the Columbine High School massacre in Littleton, Colorado.[2]

I met a man who was converted because of a Rolling Stones rock concert. In his youth he didn't believe that Satan existed. Consequently, he felt no need of Jesus Christ. His hero was Mick Jagger, lead singer of the Rolling Stones. But at the concert he attended, amid the seismic, decibel-defying clamor of the "music," the young man heard a voice that he recognized as belonging to Satan. The voice said, "You're mine, and I'm going to kill you!" Terrified, he was unable to party after the concert. Instead, he found his grandmother's copy of *The Great Controversy* by Ellen G. White and read it. He gave his life to Jesus Christ and became a minister of His gospel. Satan had scared him out of hell!

Many people today deny the existence of Satan. Therefore they don't recognize the nature of the great war or their need to be saved from evil by their loving Creator, who originated only good and who has given His life to save them. But those who are in closest touch with Satan know that he is real and that he is bitterly opposed to the God of the Bible.

In a terrifying book about deliverance from the occult titled *He Came to Set the Captives Free,* Rebecca Brown relates the life of a former witch, a satanic high priestess who was at one time the top "bride" of Satan in the United States, who was delivered from appalling degradation when she accepted Christ. To Brown, the ex-witch graphically described monstrous, giant demons who could tear a person apart; ritual sex orgies; a Black Sabbath (or Black Mass) that involved crucifixion of a man to mock the crucifixion of Christ; and the attempt of satanists to carry out Satan's order to murder a family of Christians who were interfering with Satan by converting some cult members to Christ.

Surrounding the property of the Christians was a ring of huge "link angels" from God, with no weapons or armor. The satanists repeatedly tried to break through the cordon, but they could not. Weapons bounced off the angels, who simply laughed. And when the angels merely changed the expression on their faces to a fierce look, the powerful satanists fell back helpless onto the ground.[3] As the apostle Paul put it, "If God is for us, who can be against us?" (Romans 8:31, NKJV).

The human role in the great war

Paul recognized that by ourselves, we are helpless: "We do not wrestle against flesh and blood, but against principalities, against powers, against the rulers of the darkness of this age, against spiritual hosts of wickedness in the heavenly places" (Ephesians 6:12, NKJV). But if we are with God, the forces of evil are helpless: "I am persuaded that neither death nor life, nor angels nor principalities nor powers, nor things present nor things to come, nor height nor depth, nor any other created thing, shall be able to separate us from the love of God which is in Christ Jesus our Lord" (Romans 8:38, 39, NKJV).

If the power of God and His angels is so much greater than that of the enemy forces, why didn't the great war end long ago? Shouldn't overwhelming military superiority ensure a quick victory, like the Blitzkrieg of 1939–40 or Operation Desert Storm of 1991? What is holding things up?

The answer is found in the role of human beings in the great war. We have been pawns of Satan. God cannot "nuke" all evil without exterminating people whom He is trying to rescue. If we were simply kidnapped or hijacked, God would have no problem. His angels could invade the kingdom of darkness the way commandos freed hostages from an Air France jetliner in Entebbe, Uganda, in 1976. God's challenge is that human beings have chosen Satan's kingdom.

According to the book of Genesis, God gave the dominion of this world to Adam and Eve, the first human beings (Genesis 1:28). But by following the voice of evil in rebellion against God, they fell under the control of Satan, who became " 'the ruler of this world' " (John 12:31). This explains why the book of Job describes Satan as showing up among the "sons of God" to present himself before the Lord (Job 1:6). Because Adam and Eve had elected him to the heavenly congress, Satan could claim to represent planet Earth in place of them.

Satan lost his seat in congress when Jesus Christ, a descendant of Adam and Eve, regained dominion for the human race. As Creator of the world, Christ had always been the Sovereign of planet Earth. That is why Satan tempted Him to avoid suffering by simply reversing the hierarchy of authority, putting Satan in first place instead of Himself. But Christ knew that if He worshiped Satan, all human beings would be lost. If the Most High gave in to the one who coveted His place, He would no longer be the Most High and He couldn't save us. Rather, Christ the Creator chose to become a human being and live a life of total loyalty to God—thereby succeeding where Adam and Eve had failed—and to pay the painful penalty for the disobedience of the human race. In this way He "judged" the world in the positive sense of gaining justice for planet Earth by casting out Satan, the oppressive, foreign usurper (John 12:31; compare the judges, or deliverers, of the book of Judges).[4]

A couple questions arise. First, why didn't God simply destroy the human race when Adam and Eve decided to follow Satan instead of Him?

God didn't destroy Adam and Even because they didn't fully understand what they were doing. Eve was deceived, and Adam didn't grasp the big picture. They were like inexperienced children who disregard a warning without comprehending the consequences. Do we kill our children when they disobey us and get into big trouble?

Second, why didn't the great war end two thousand years ago when Christ cast out Satan at the Cross? Hadn't John the Baptist and Jesus proclaimed, " 'Repent, for the kingdom of heaven is at hand' " (Matthew 3:2; 4:17)?

Christ's victory on the cross was like D-Day in 1944, when the Allies gained a foothold on the continent of Europe and practically ensured that Hitler's days were numbered. In fact, the outcome of the great war is absolutely assured: Good will inevitably triumph over evil. However, the fighting goes on and even increases in intensity because many human beings still prefer the lordship of Satan. They choose him because he continues to cruelly deceive them into thinking that God doesn't want the best for them and that they aren't accountable to Him. Therefore, they believe that they can provide for their own happiness better than God can by being free to be self-ish and worship themselves. The lie is an old one. In fact, it is what the satanic serpent promised Eve in the Garden of Eden: " 'You will not surely die. For God knows that in the day you eat of it your eyes will be opened, and you will be like God, knowing good and evil' " (Genesis 3:4, 5, NKJV).

Having aspired to take the place of God, Satan tries to pass his dream of being "like God" on to us in order to make us little satans. If he has failed at taking God's place even though he was the mighty covering cherub, what makes us think we can succeed—mortal flesh and blood that we are?

We have found that there is a great war between God and Satan over rulership of this world. The disputed issue is the character of God and whether anyone should take His place. In the remaining chapters of this book, we will explore the way in which God demonstrates His fairness when He saves or condemns human beings in accordance with their choices for or against Him. When this "judgment" is complete, no more questions about God's character will remain and nobody will be lost who otherwise could be saved. At that point, no further delay will be needed, and God can swiftly move to end the great war.

---

1. Regarding the profound impact of World War II on worldviews, see Margaret Mead, "Family System and Society," in *Changing Sexual Values and the Family*, G. Pirozo Sholevar, ed. (Springfield, Ill.: Charles C. Thomas, 1977), 33–35.

2. Adam Cohen, "A Curse of Cliques," *Time*, May 3, 1999, 45.

3. Rebecca Brown, *He Came to Set the Captives Free* (New Kensington, Penn.: Whitaker House, 1992), 56, 57.

4. Roy Gane, *God's Faulty Heroes* (Hagerstown, Md.: Review and Herald, 1996), 44.

Judgments to Demonstrate God's Character

On a plane trip to the country of Jordan to participate in an archaeological excavation, my wife and I sat behind a young man and began to chat with him. He was a soldier from an elite military unit on a two-week leave from a long and grueling tour of duty in Iraq. He was dreading going back; tears came to his eyes as he painfully recounted that his buddy had just been shot in the neck by a sniper. Such men and women do not get to choose whether they live or die.

In the great war, who decides whether we are saved or lost? We do! In that sense, we judge ourselves. This is great news. God is the ultimate Judge, but He gives all of us the opportunity to choose what we want, and He accepts our decisions. When we say to Him, "Yes, Your Honor"—when we accept the gospel, the good news about Him—it is as though we're ruling in favor of ourselves because we've allied ourselves with Him.

It was that way in the time of Noah. God gave people plenty of opportunity to understand and accept the good news that they could escape the coming Flood. The door of the ark was open to everyone. God didn't force a single person on or off the boat. When the door of the ark was shut, the destinies of people were fixed according to the decisions they had made (Genesis 6; 7). Whether or not they were saved was up to them, but they had to choose to be saved through the provision that God had made. Anyone who said No to God forfeited

17

His protection when He unleashed His watery weapon of mass destruction against the domain of Satan and his followers.

Satan accuses God of being unfair, but it is God who respects human free choice. The divine risen Christ says, " ' "Behold, I stand at the door and knock; if anyone hears My voice and opens the door, I will come in to him, and will dine with him, and he with Me" ' " (Revelation 3:20). If anyone has the right to force his way into our lives, Christ does—the One who created us and died for us. But He stands outside the door of the human heart and asks to come in, and only if we respond will He enter.

Hypocritically, it is Satan who doesn't respect free choice. God warned jealous Cain when he was contemplating evil against his brother, " 'If you do not do well, sin is crouching at the door; and its desire is for you' " (Genesis 4:7). Sin and Satan don't knock. "Sin is crouching at the door" means that moral evil is just waiting for an opportunity to burst in like a predatory animal and take over the heart. The words "its desire is for you" don't mean that sin is like a sweet kitty that wants to climb on your lap and purr. They mean that sin is like a saber-toothed tiger that likes you in the sense that it wants to gobble you up.

In Jesus' day, demonic spirits possessed many people. These people were deeply grateful when Jesus and His disciples delivered them. Obviously, Satan and his fallen angels had no respect for the wishes of their victims, or the evil spirits would not have come uninvited or worn out their wicked welcome.

According to the Bible, God is fair in the sense that He allows people to choose. He appeals, explains, and warns of the positive and negative consequences that the "way of life" and the "way of death" bring (Jeremiah 21:8), but He doesn't force anyone to be saved or lost. If He used force, why would He go to the trouble of appealing to people's hearts?

God is also completely fair when He holds people accountable for their choices. The Bible says, " 'He will judge the peoples with equity.' . . . [F]or He is coming to judge the earth. He will judge the world in righteousness, and the peoples in His faithfulness" (Psalm 96:10, 13).

By contrast, human judges and courts can make mistakes. Lindy Chamberlain, an Adventist pastor's wife, was accused of murdering her baby while she and her husband were camping in the middle of Australia. At the conclusion of the most famous trial in Australian legal history, Lindy was convicted and imprisoned. After a time of intense pain for her and her family, it was shown that the investigation by the Northern Territories police was flawed and that a dingo (a kind of wild Australian dog) had in fact killed the baby.

Human courts can go wrong even when they are trying to be fair and even when they assemble all available evidence and use unbiased juries. But God has the ultimate advantage: " 'the LORD searches all hearts, and understands every intent of the thoughts' " (1 Chronicles 28:9).

To make sure we understand that God's verdicts are fair, the Bible repeatedly describes Him as judging by perceiving, investigating, and assessing situations before He carries out punishment or allows penalties of justice to fall.[1] Thus, for example, before He destroyed the world with a great flood, "the LORD *saw* that the wickedness of man was great on the earth, and that every intent of the thoughts of his heart was only evil continually" (Genesis 6:5, emphasis supplied). In the Tower of Babel story, "the LORD came down to see the city and the tower which the sons of men had built" (Genesis 11:5). Before He destroyed Sodom and Gomorrah, "the LORD said, 'The outcry of Sodom and Gomorrah is indeed great, and their sin is exceedingly grave. I will go down now, and see if they have done entirely according to its outcry, which has come to Me; and if not, I will know' " (Genesis 18:20, 21).

God's full disclosure

It is one thing to believe the Bible when it portrays God as fair, but it is another thing to feel comfortable with the results of God's judgment, especially when the results are so radically different: eternal life or eternal death. Nowhere in the judicial system of any country are there such extreme rewards or punishments. If you love someone dearly and expect to see that person in heaven but he or she doesn't show up there, how will you react—especially if you find that your worst enemy *is* there? In spite of your strong faith, you might be tempted to doubt that God had acted with perfect justice.

Such doubts could be dangerous and lead to another rebellion in the future. To guarantee eternal security, God needs to settle all such doubts so that sin will not arise a second time. He wants to do the job properly the first time (see Nahum 1:9). How can He do it? Obviously, the solution would be for Him to allow everyone who will continue to live in His universe to examine all the evidence on which He based His verdicts. This would be a remarkable level of full disclosure, even for a mere earthly ruler. Can you imagine all branches of your government making all of their records available to the entire public—even declassifying sensitive material?

According to the Bible, God indeed opens His records to His created beings. He does this in two stages of what can be called "judgment." First, the records (the Bible calls them books) are opened in heaven before Christ comes to earth a second time. " 'I kept looking until thrones were set up, and the Ancient of Days took His seat; His vesture was like white snow, and the hair of His head like pure wool. His throne was ablaze with flames, its wheels were a burning fire. A river of fire was flowing and coming out from before Him; thousands upon thousands were attending Him, and myriads upon myriads were standing before Him; the court sat, and the books were opened' " (Daniel 7:9, 10).

In chapter 4 we will study this passage in detail, but for now, it is enough to recognize that this event informs those of God's created beings who are in heaven. These would include mostly various kinds of what we would call "angels" (including cherubim and seraphim). However, Christ represents the human race in heaven (in addition to Enoch, Moses, and Elisha, whom God took to heaven—see Daniel 17:13, " 'One like a Son of Man,' " and see Genesis 5:24; 2 Kings 2:11; Matthew 17:3; Jude 9). The "twenty-four elders" of Revelation 4:4 may also be redeemed human beings who rose to life at the time of Christ's death (Matthew 27:52, 53).

Second, there is another phase of judgment in heaven during the thousand years after Christ's second coming:

> I saw thrones, and they sat upon them, and judgment was given to them. And I saw the souls of those who had been beheaded because of the testimony of Jesus and because of the word of God, and those who had not worshiped the beast or his image, and had not received the mark upon their forehead and upon their hand; and they came to life and reigned

with Christ for a thousand years. . . . And I saw a great white throne and Him who sat upon it, from whose presence earth and heaven fled away, and no place was found for them. And I saw the dead, the great and the small, standing before the throne, and books were opened; and another book was opened, which is the book of life; and the dead were judged from the things which were written in the books, according to their deeds (Revelation 20:4, 11, 12).

This time the process involves the large group of saved human beings who are taken to heaven at the resurrection when Christ comes again (see 1 Thessalonians 4:16, 17).

Why must there be two stages of judgment? Both stages are in heaven, where God's headquarters are located and where His records are kept. The vast majority of saved human beings cannot participate in a judgment in heaven before Christ's second coming because they are on earth. So God gives them the opportunity to examine His records in a second stage of judgment when they get to heaven.

Daniel 7 and Revelation 20 refer to "books" that are used for the first and second stages of judgment. We don't know the precise nature of these archives. Perhaps if Daniel or John were writing today they would refer to "DVDs" or "databases." But use of such records clearly implies some kind of investigation. However, here is a crucial point: *God Himself doesn't really need a public investigative judgment for His own information.* As the Divine Judge, God already knows everything (see, for example, Psalm 139) and can determine the fates of those who are saved or lost on His own, without help from angels or redeemed human beings. So if we refer to the event in Daniel 7 as an "investigative judgment," we mean that God allows His created beings to investigate what He already knows. From His perspective, it is a "demonstrative judgment"—in it, the facts of each case are demonstrated.

There is a key difference between the use of "books" and the investigations God carried out before He acted at the Flood, the Tower of Babel, and Sodom and Gomorrah (see above). Scripture pictures God as checking these latter situations in order to make a decision before applying His judgments. True, He really knew what was going on all along, but the Bible portrays Him as going through

21

the motions of investigation so that human beings can understand that He is fair. Use of "books" or records, on the other hand, implies that God has already assessed the situations, which means that His own investigations have already taken place. To use an analogy, if you read your diary to someone, you are sharing ideas you have already thought and expressed.

The second stage of judgment during the thousand years after Christ's second coming doesn't fix any verdicts in the sense of deciding whether people are saved or lost. Christ brings His final rewards with Him when He comes (Revelation 22:12; cp. Matthew 25:31–46), which means that after this point there is no determining whether a person is saved or lost. It appears that after God takes the saved to heaven, they judge in the sense of being involved in the process of fixing the severity of ultimate penalties administered at the end of the thousand years to those who are lost (degrees of suffering at the second death in the lake of fire). Notice that this "hell" event destroys Satan, who has no control over hell whatsoever. It is clear that the redeemed will have full knowledge of God's reasons for what He does and will be convinced of His justice.

Final confirmation that God is right will come when "at the name of Jesus *every* knee should bow, of those who are in heaven, and on earth, and under the earth, and . . . *every* tongue should confess that Jesus Christ is Lord, to the glory of God the Father" (Philippians 2:10, 11, emphasis supplied). Agreement even by those who are punished testifies to the justice of a sentence like nothing else (see Judges 1:7).

---

1. John T. Anderson, *Investigating the Judgment* (Hagerstown, Md.: Review and Herald, 2003), 62–76, 85–95, 100–104; Gerhard Pfandl, *Daniel: The Seer of Babylon* (Hagerstown, Md.: Review and Herald, 2004), 69–71. On biblical parallels for the investigative judgment, see also William H. Shea, *Selected Studies on Prophetic Interpretation*, Daniel and Revelation Committee Series 1, Frank H. Holbrook, ed. (Silver Spring, Md.: Biblical Research Institute, 1992), 1–29.

CHAPTER 3

Covenant, Character, and History

Anyone who has been married for several years can tell you that a close relationship between two people changes through time. A marriage can last for well over half a century, but it doesn't stay the same; the relationship develops for better or worse as the partners face situations together and interact with each other. Their relationship may grow deeper, more meaningful, and more tender, or it may sink into distrust, abuse, and misery. It can shift nearly imperceptibly, or it may undergo sudden jolts due to major events, such as the birth of a child, a change of occupation or location, an accident, or adultery.

A marriage is a story or private history involving two characters. The story has a beginning (wedding) and an end (death or divorce), between which it moves from one day to another and from one year to another. The present is always moving ahead, so that what is future becomes present and then past. Although some elements of the story can recur, as when a succession of children go through similar stages, the overall story is a forward progression.

The covenant relationship between God and His people is like a marriage (see Hosea; Ezekiel 16) in that it develops through time as the human partners change in their attitudes toward Him and in their character. God's overall character of love remains the same, but to nurture His relationship with faulty human beings in order to save them, He adjusts His approach to fit their needs. Thus, when Solomon was young and faithful, God blessed him with all kinds of fabulous benefits

(1 Kings 3–10). But when he turned from the Lord through polygamy that led him into idolatry, God began to weaken and reduce his kingdom (1 Kings 11). Similarly, when the Israelites apostatized during the period of the judges, the Lord let them try to bumble along by themselves without His protection (see, for example, Judges 10). But when they returned to Him, "He could bear the misery of Israel no longer" (Judges 10:16) and felt compelled to help them.

Because God is the superior, more mature partner who needs to discipline His people for their good, the covenant can also be compared to a parent-child relationship: "Those whom the Lord loves He disciplines. . . . God deals with you as with sons; for what son is there whom his father does not discipline? . . . He disciplines us for our good, that we may share His holiness. All discipline for the moment seems not to be joyful, but sorrowful; yet to those who have been trained by it, afterwards it yields the peaceful fruit of righteousness" (Hebrews 12:6, 7, 10, 11).

Solomon was an heir not only of the Lord's covenant with Israel at Sinai, but also of His royal covenant with David and his descendants. Of this covenant, God promised: " 'If his sons forsake My law, and do not walk in My judgments, if they violate My statutes, and do not keep My commandments, then I will visit their transgression with the rod, and their iniquity with stripes. But I will not break off My lovingkindness from him, nor deal falsely in My faithfulness' " (Psalm 89:30–33).

By rewarding loyalty and by exercising tough love through painful correction when it was necessary, God sought to preserve His people and enhance their relationship with Him so they could receive the blessings He had promised. If He didn't discipline them when they veered into destructive patterns of behavior, He would be responsible for encouraging them in a downward spiral that would hurt them and others, as Eli was to blame when he neglected to put a stop to the reckless behavior of his sons Hophni and Phinehas (1 Samuel 2–4).

Excellence for evangelism

God's sensible instructions and His rewards and punishments for keeping or disobeying them (compare the blessings and curses in Leviticus 26 and Deuteronomy 28) are not merely for the sake of

His people. Their larger purpose is to teach other groups what He is like so that they can be drawn to Him. Moses charged the Israelites: " 'See, I have taught you statutes and judgments just as the LORD my God commanded me, that you should do thus in the land where you are entering to possess it. So keep and do them, for that is your wisdom and your understanding in the sight of the peoples who will hear all these statutes and say, "Surely this great nation is a wise and understanding people." For what great nation is there that has a god so near to it as is the LORD our God whenever we call on Him? Or what great nation is there that has statutes and judgments as righteous as this whole law which I am setting before you today?' " (Deuteronomy 4:5–8).

Fulfilling this promise, God drew the queen of Sheba to Himself through the wisdom and wealth that He had given to Solomon (1 Kings 10). *And God wants nothing more than to lavish all kinds of blessings on His people today so that others will see His power and love and want to belong to Him too.* But if He were to bless them when they defy His leadership, guidance, and laws of cause and effect, He would defeat His purpose and repel others by sending the signal that He supports evil.

The implications and applications of the biblical principles just stated are of staggering significance. Through Christ, we are all heirs of the Lord's covenant with Abraham (Galatians 3:29), to whom God promised: " 'I will bless you, and make your name great; and so you shall be a blessing; and I will bless those who bless you, and the one who curses you I will curse. *And in you all the families of the earth shall be blessed'* " (Genesis 12:2, 3, emphasis supplied). God wants to prosper us, to make us in every way " 'the head and not the tail' " (Deuteronomy 28:13), but it is not simply for our benefit. Rather, it is so that God can use us as channels of blessing to all peoples, to draw them to Himself.

At the annual Midwest Region meeting of the Society of Biblical Literature, awards are given to graduate students who submit the best research papers in the areas of Old Testament and New Testament. In 2005, both awards went to Ph.D. in religion students from the Seventh-day Adventist Theological Seminary at Andrews University. The scholars who chose the winners told me that they had noticed the coincidence and were a bit perplexed. But they had decided that these two students should be honored even though they came from the same school because they had clearly produced the best papers. The scholars also remarked that good things must be happening at Andrews. When I learned to whom the awards were going, I was immensely proud of our students and thrilled that God is blessing our efforts to produce excellence for Him. Most exhilarating, however, is the privilege of participating with God as He uses *the influence of excellence for His glory.*

Excellence is for evangelism! Development of ourselves and our community in accordance with divine principles is essential for fulfilling Christ's great commission to take His gospel to the whole world. When people see how healthy, happy, and prosperous we are, we have a golden (or platinum!) opportunity to tell them that our God is the greatest. When we excel in education, wisdom, and skill, we can point to the divine Source of all knowledge and understanding. When our families are more harmonious, our divorce rates are lower, and our church unity is uniquely strong, we can lead them to the Messiah, who prayed for those who believe in Him " 'that they all may be one, as You, Father, are in Me, and I in You; that they also may be one in Us, that the world may believe that You sent Me. And the glory which You gave Me I have given them, that they may be one just as We are one: I in them, and You in Me; that they may be made perfect in one, and *that the world may know that You have sent Me,* and have loved them as You have loved Me' " (John 17:21–23, NKJV; emphasis supplied).

On the other hand, when we are sloppy, self-indulgent, and selfish regarding our health, relationships, study, and work so that our bodies, our marriages and other relationships, and our academic and professional performance are little or no better than those of the general population, why should others be interested? Who is attracted to mediocrity? If we don't care, why should they?

If we do prosper but fail to give God the credit, we short-circuit evangelism as Hezekiah did when he showed the Babylonian envoys his riches without mentioning their Source. Like Hezekiah, we may find it dangerous when people covet our earthly advantages rather than seek the Lord who gave them (Isaiah 39).

When *Apollo 13* was crippled by an explosion on the way to the moon, placing the lives of three astronauts in critical jeopardy, Gene

Kranz, the flight director of Mission Control in Houston, was determined to get them back safely. He is reported to have said to his team, "Failure is not an option!" For Christians, mediocrity is failure, and it is not an option.

The essence of biblical history is the story of God's relationship with His people, which shows how His character was revealed and how theirs developed one way or another. Biblical history also includes chronology, archival lists, geographic data, reports of military and building activities, and so on. However, although these kinds of things can be of considerable interest to us, their function is to provide background for the central story that teaches us what God is like and how we should relate to Him.

Covenant history and God's character in Daniel

A particularly powerful part of God's covenant story is found in the book of Daniel. Daniel 1:1, 2 says that *"the Lord gave* Jehoiakim king of Judah" into the hand of Nebuchadnezzar, king of Babylon (emphasis supplied). Then Nebuchadnezzar ordered that some young men from the royal family and nobles of Judah be brought to Babylon, in order to train them for his service. Among these were Daniel and his friends (verses 3–6). Thus was fulfilled Isaiah's prediction to Hezekiah, after he bragged about himself rather than God to the Babylonian envoys: " ' "Some of your sons who shall issue from you, whom you shall beget, shall be taken away; and they shall become officials in the palace of the king of Babylon" ' " (Isaiah 39:7). So covenant failure on the part of God's people and their leaders led to exile.

In striking contrast, the courageous covenant loyalty of Daniel and his friends allowed God to bless them in stunning ways. Even in exile, they were "the head and not the tail," and their excellence evangelized emperors (Daniel 1–6).

The prophecies of the book of Daniel amplify the message of the stories, which is encapsulated in the repeated refrain that " ' "the Most High rules in the kingdom of men, [and] gives it to whomever He will" ' " (Daniel 4:17, NKJV; see also verses 25, 32; 5:21). In Daniel 2, the first of these prophecies appears in the form of a divinely induced dream given to Nebuchadnezzar near the beginning of his reign and interpreted by Daniel.

Three earthly empires would follow Nebuchadnezzar's Neo-Babylonian kingdom, which was represented by the golden head of an awesome statue. In the dream, these empires were symbolized by progressively lower portions of the body of the same image, made of metals with decreasing value but increasing hardness: silver, bronze, and iron. The iron power would last until the end, but in its final phase it would be divided and weakened, as shown by its mixture with clay (verses 31–33, 36–43). The climax of the prophecy is the divine destruction of the human kingdoms, represented by a stone that has been cut out without hands that then strikes the bottom of the image. God's eternal kingdom, which the stone symbolizes, replaces the earthly empires and fills the whole earth (verses 34, 35, 44, 45).

Notice the following defining characteristics of this prophecy in Daniel 2, which sets the agenda for later prophecies in the book of Daniel (chapters 7–12):

1. The prophecy outlines history of planet Earth that was future from Daniel's perspective. Daniel explicitly explained to Nebuchadnezzar that " 'the great God has made known to the king what will take place in the future' " (verse 45). The message is not a spiritualized abstraction, but has to do with real nations and their rulers, whose achievements and exploits would be recorded in later books of secular history. So the accuracy or inaccuracy of the prophecy could ultimately be tested.

2. The "classical" prophecies of the other prophetic books in the Old Testament deliver divine messages (warning, appeal, comfort, etc.) to localized groups of people living in particular time periods. Unlike those prophecies, this one in Daniel 2 covers an immense sweep of history stretching from the time of the prophet all the way to the worldwide end of human civilization as we know it. Since the cosmic end has not yet occurred, the prophecy must reach through our time. It is not all in the past or all in the future, but the present keeps moving forward.

3. The sweep of history is presented as continuous. It doesn't start in ancient times, then skip over hundreds or thousands of years, and resume with events just before God puts an end to earthly rule and takes over.

4. There is only one interpretation. While the prophecy is highly symbolic, a given symbol stands for only one reality. For example,

the head of gold represents only Nebuchadnezzar, that is, Nebu-chadnezzar's kingdom (verses 37, 38).

5. The overall point of the prophecy is the same as the central theme of the book of Daniel as a whole: "The Most High rules in the kingdom of men" (see Daniel 4:17, etc., and see above). So the message is a revelation of who God is and what He is like as shown by what He does in relation to human beings and their history. He possesses sovereign power over planet Earth, which He will fully exercise once He has allowed earthly rule to run its course.

From the perspective of Daniel in exile, whose fellow Jews—the covenant people—were being oppressed by Babylon, the first of four great empires, the prophecy was wonderfully good news. God would eventually stop repressive regimes and take over direct rulership of the world forever. This implies that in the future, His covenant people will dwell with Him in eternal peace and security. The story of their relationship with Him will have a good ending: God will rule wisely and well, and they will live happily ever after.

CHAPTER 4

Judgment of the Loyal and Disloyal (Daniel 7)

Many years after Daniel interpreted the dream of Nebuchadnezzar, he had a prophetic dream that covered the sweep of history from his time to the end (Daniel 7). This time the symbols of successive empires were moving animals rather than motionless parts of a statue. The prophecy, with its interpretation, added some important details not found in Nebuchadnezzar's dream, thereby contributing to our understanding of the character of the "Most High" and the way He "rules in the kingdom of men."

Like Daniel 2, Daniel 7 predicted four great kings/kingdoms (Daniel 7:17), which would be terminated and superseded by God's eternal kingdom. In Daniel 7, the explicit emphasis is on the benefit to God's people, who would receive the kingdom of this world (verse 18). As in Daniel 2, Daniel 7 portrays a transformation of the fourth earthly empire, which is the strongest. However, whereas in Daniel 2 the fourth kingdom is only weakened and divided (verses 41–43), in Daniel 7 a "different" power represented by a horn that starts out "little" arises from the fourth empire. This "little-horn" power has a religious agenda: It arrogantly affronts God by speaking against Him, attempting to change His times and law and persecuting His faithful people for a specified period, namely, three and one-half "times" (verses 8, 20, 21, 24, 25).

The biggest new element introduced in Daniel 7 is an awesome divine judgment that precedes the destruction of human rule and transfer of power to God and His people (verses 9–14, 22, 26, 27). In the New Testament, we see that the Lord's defeat of an arrogant, blasphemous power that opposes His authority and law and His conquest of planet Earth occurs at His second coming (2 Thessalonians 2:1–12; see also Revelation 13; 19:11–21). In this light, it is clear that Daniel 7 presents a pre-Advent judgment.

Like Daniel 2, Daniel 7 explicitly interprets its symbolism as presenting real human history that begins with the time of Daniel and moves into the future: " ' "Those great beasts, which are four, are four kings which arise out of the earth" ' " (verse 17, NKJV). Since the sweep of history from Daniel's time to the end is continuous, it must include our time. This historicist understanding of the prophecy emerges from the way in which the biblical text presents and explains itself. This is in contrast to "preterist" (past) and "futurist" (including dispensational) approaches that impose methodological assumptions on the biblical text. Preterism and futurism leave gaps by avoiding application of the prophecy to certain historical eras (especially the Middle Ages) through artificially lumping fulfillments into the past (especially the second century B.C. time of the Seleucid king Antiochus IV Epiphanes) or into the distant future (future antichrist, etc.).[1]

It is well recognized that Old Testament prophecy and theology in general are rooted in history as a continuum, as contrasted with the cyclical approach of the ancient Egyptians and Mesopotamians. Historicists, preterists, and futurists agree that the book of Daniel contains history and eschatology (prophecy of the end time). The question is where history ends and prediction begins in relation to the time of the author of Daniel.

Historicists take the text as it reads: Daniel predicts a stream of events from his time in the sixth century B.C. to the second coming of Christ. Preterists, who tend to deny the possibility of divinely authored, accurate prediction, regard Daniel's "prophecies" as a combination of accurate historical records written in the second century B.C. *after* the events they describe had occurred (culminating in the persecution conducted by Antiochus IV Epiphanes), plus inaccurate prediction of what the second-century author (not a sixth-century B.C. Daniel who lived at the time of the Neo-Babylonian Empire) supposed would happen in the future. Futurists stay with

31

the historicists and/or preterists up to a point in the flow of predicted events, after which they jump to the end time. Futurists often detach the final week from the seventy-weeks prophecy of Daniel 9:24–27 and thrust its fulfillment forward to the latter days.[2]

What difference does it make whether you are a historicist, preterist, or futurist? For one thing, this choice determines your understanding of the way in which Daniel's prophecies are fulfilled, which shapes the way you personally relate to their messages. If you are a preterist, you lack the assurance that the Driver of the universe can see in advance where He is going, but you don't need to worry about the dangerous power represented by the little horn, nor is the judgment on it in Daniel 7 relevant to you, because these things were fulfilled twenty-two centuries ago in the time of Antiochus IV Epiphanes. On the other hand, if you are a futurist, you may wonder who the future antichrist (fulfillment of the little horn) will be, but you can't really identify him now and you think the judgment on him is somewhere off in the future.

By contrast, if you are a historicist, you may find that an identifiable little-horn power is still here and God's pre-Advent judgment may be going on right now! So you may be faced with a choice for God or for His enemy, and this choice will fix your eternal destiny, as determined in the judgment (compare Revelation 13; 14)! If you miss this by looking in the past or future for what is really present, as I once searched everywhere for the glasses that were on my face, you may misunderstand the nature of God's judgment and character, and you may be unprepared to make the right choice with regard to Him. As a result, you may face consequences that you would rather avoid, to say the least.

Identifying the little-horn power

How do we identify the power represented by the little horn? To begin with, we need to trace the succession of four earlier kingdoms, which parallel the four kingdoms in Daniel 2. The first animal in Daniel 7 is the lion (verse 4), which corresponds to the gold head in Daniel 2. Daniel identified this animal as representing Nebuchadnezzar's Neo-Babylonian kingdom (verses 37, 38). Beast number two in Daniel 7, which corresponds to the silver chest and arms in Daniel 2:32, is a lopsided bear (7:5), which represents the empire that superseded Babylon. In the narratives of Daniel 5 and 6 and in secular history, this was the combined kingdom of Media-Persia, which conquered Babylon in 539 B.C.

The third animal is a leopard (Daniel 7:6), which corresponds to the belly and thighs of bronze in Daniel 2:32. It must represent the Macedonian-Greek Empire of Alexander the Great, who conquered Media-Persia before his untimely death in 323 B.C. at the age of thirty-two. Supporting this identification are the four wings and heads of the leopard, which agree with the fact that after Alexander's death, his empire split into four Hellenistic kingdoms: Antigonid Macedonia, Attalid Pergamum, Seleucid Syria, and Ptolemaic Egypt. Further confirmation is found in Daniel 8, where the kingdom of Greece under its first king (that is, Alexander) conquers the kingdom of Media and Persia. These powers are explicitly named in verses 20, 21.

Thus far, the succession of empires is clear and verifiable both within Daniel and in secular history. There remains the fourth kingdom, symbolized by iron legs in Daniel 2:33 and by a powerful, frightful monster with iron teeth and ten horns in Daniel 7:7. Notice that the common feature of iron links the two representations. We know from the New Testament and from secular history which power superseded the four Greek kingdoms: imperial Rome, which was the strongest, most oppressive, and most enduring of all the four empires.

If the four wings and heads of the Greek leopard (chapter 7:6) symbolize the breakup of Alexander's empire into four parts, it would make sense that the ten horns of the Roman monster (verse 7) represent the division of this empire into ten parts. This is in harmony with the explanation in Daniel 2:41 that the feet and toes of iron and clay stand for a divided kingdom. Again, secular history testifies to the accuracy of the prophecy: In the fifth century A.D., the western Roman Empire was taken over by several Germanic tribes.

Daniel 7:8 says, " 'While I was contemplating the horns, behold, another horn, a little one, came up among them, and three of the first horns were pulled out by the roots before it; and behold, this horn possessed eyes like the eyes of a man, and a mouth uttering great boasts.' " The first words of this verse, referring to Daniel looking at the ten horns, implies that the religiously oriented little horn was to arise from the division of imperial Rome. What power like this developed from Rome soon after it was divided? There is only one viable answer: The Church of Rome, which arose at the expense of some Germanic tribal nations that had taken over part of the Roman Empire (see Daniel 7:8, 20—three horns uprooted before the little horn), and which dominated Europe during the Middle Ages.[3]

Little horn versus holy ones

The pre-Advent judgment in Daniel 7 accomplishes two things. First, it condemns the rebellious little-horn power (verse 11). Second, it rules in favor of God's true followers, called "holy ones of the Most High," who receive the kingdom of this world (verse 22, NRSV) under the lordship of the "One like a Son of Man" (or "one like a human being," NRSV) (verses 13, 14). So the case to be judged is "little horn" versus "holy ones of the Most High." These are opposing parties, as shown by the fact that the little horn persecutes the holy ones (verses 21, 25; compare 8:10, 24, 25). The question in the judgment is: To whom does the dominion of this world rightfully belong? The verdict: It belongs to the holy ones. The little horn loses.

Some interpreters regard the books of record opened in the judgment (Daniel 7:10) as dealing exclusively with the sins of the little-horn power. Others see these books as consisting only of records of the forgiven sins of the holy ones. Both views are half right because the judgment is concerned with two groups. God is shown to be just both when He vindicates those who truly follow Him and when He condemns apostate rebels. The judgment is like the ancient Israelite Day of Atonement, which cleansed/vindicated those loyal to God (Leviticus 16:30) but condemned those who showed themselves to be disloyal (23:29, 30).

In Daniel 7:9, 10, the judgment comes after the period of domination by the little horn (compare verse 8) and takes place where the "Ancient of Days"—clearly referring to the God of heaven—is located, in heaven. There is no mention of the second coming of Christ to earth in these verses.

Linking the three scenes of verses 9–14 is the verdict resulting from the investigation (verses 9, 10) that wipes out the little-horn power (verse 11) and gives the "One like a Son of Man" an eternal kingdom (verses 13, 14). The One like a Son of Man is a heavenly person like a human being, whose coronation takes place in heaven.

Judgment of the Loyal and Disloyal (Daniel 7)

Compare verses 22, 26, 27, which emphasize that the judgment results in the demise of the little horn and God's grant of dominion to His holy ones, who in this context are human beings who have accepted the lordship of God and the One like a Son of Man.

The One like a Son of Man must be Christ, because He has divine attributes and controls an eternal kingdom that is identified as the kingdom of God in Daniel 2:44, and yet the Ancient of Days gives Him His power, so He is distinct from God the Father. Jesus frequently referred to Himself as the "Son of Man" (Matthew 8:20; 9:6; 10:23, etc.), thereby identifying Himself with the Messianic One like a Son of Man in Daniel 7.

It would be strange for an ordinary human being to commonly refer to himself as a "son of man," which means simply "human being." This is so obvious that it goes without saying. It makes sense, however, for God to address the prophet Ezekiel as "son of man" (Ezekiel 2:1, 3, 6, 8, etc.) in order to emphasize his humanness in contrast to the Lord's divinity. When Jesus Christ called Himself "Son of Man," He was emphasizing His humanity in contrast to His own divinity. It was as if Jesus were saying that the most unusual thing about Himself is the fact that He has joined the human race, combining human nature with His original and basic divinity (compare Micah 5:2; John 8:58).

---

1. For explanation of and comparison between historicism and other approaches, see, for example, *The Seventh-day Adventist Bible Commentary*, Francis D. Nichol, ed. (Hagerstown, Md.: Review and Herald, 1955), 4:42; Gerhard F. Hasel, "Interpretation of the Chronology of the Seventy Weeks," in *The Seventy Weeks, Leviticus, and the Nature of Prophecy*, Daniel and Revelation Committee Series 3, Frank H. Holbrook, ed. (Silver Spring, Md.: Biblical Research Institute, 1986), 13–63; William H. Shea, *Daniel 7–12: Prophecies of the End Time*, The Abundant Life Bible Amplifier (Nampa, Idaho: Pacific Press®, 1996), 33–46; Jon Paulien, "The End of Historicism? Reflections on the Adventist Approach to Biblical Apocalyptic—Part One," *Journal of the Adventist Theological Society* 14 (2003):15–43.

2. Regarding the futurist/dispensational approach to this passage, see Brempong Owusu-Antwi, *The Chronology of Daniel 9:24-27*, Adventist Theological Society Dissertation Series 2 (Berrien Springs, Mich.: Adventist Theological Society, 1995), 42–49.

3. See further in Roy Gane, *Altar Call* (Berrien Springs, Mich.: Diadem, 1999), 300, 301.

CHAPTER 5

Justifying God's Sanctuary and Reputation (Daniel 8)

Whereas Daniel 7 presents a grand pre-Advent judgment as the solution to the problem of the little horn, the solution in Daniel 8 is expressed differently as the justification/vindication of God's sanctuary (verse 14). We will find that the functional equivalence between these two depictions of the same event is of profound importance for grasping the way in which God preserves the reputation of His loving, holy character.

Daniel 8 parallels chapters 2 and 7 in that it covers the sweep of history from Daniel's day until the end of the present era. However, although the prophet received the vision of Daniel 8 in the third regnal year of the Babylonian king Belshazzar (co-regent with his father, Nabonidus), ominously, the vision doesn't include Babylon because this power was about to end. Rather, it begins with the progression from Media-Persia to Macedonia/Greece (explicitly identified in verses 20, 21), as symbolized by a ram followed by a he-goat (verses 3–8).

The goat's large horn (verses 5, 8) stands for the first king of the Grecian Empire (verse 21), who shattered the power of the Medo-Persian Empire. There is no question that this is Alexander the Great, whose empire was subsequently split up into four Hellenistic kingdoms, represented by four horns that came up "toward the four winds of heaven" (verses 8, 22; see also Daniel 7:6).

Daniel 8:9 introduces the next player on the scene of action: "Out of one of them came forth a rather small horn which grew exceedingly great toward the south, toward the east, and toward the Beautiful Land." This horn, which starts out little and in this sense can be called a little horn, is the same symbol used in Daniel 7. However, whereas in Daniel 7 the little horn sprouts from a monstrous beast, here in Daniel 8 the little horn comes "out of one of them," meaning out of one of the four winds of heaven. The "four winds" represent the four directions of the compass (see Jeremiah 49:36; Ezekiel 37:9; Daniel 7:2; Zechariah 2:6; Matthew 24:31; Revelation 7:1)—north, south, east, and west—into which Alexander's empire was divided.

In attempting to establish Antiochus IV Epiphanes, a Hellenistic Seleucid ruler, as the little horn, many scholars have taken "out of one of them" to mean that the little horn comes out of one of the Hellenistic horns—after all, horns do not come out of winds. But neither do horns normally grow out of other horns, and this is symbolic prophecy, where symbols need not conform to what we find in real life. For example, have you ever seen a leopard with four wings and four heads (Daniel 7:6)?

Several points justify our rejecting the interpretation that Daniel 8:9 predicts the rise and career of Antiochus:

1. The "them" in "out of one of them" at the beginning of verse 9 most naturally refers to the nearest antecedent: the immediately preceding "four winds of heaven" at the end of verse 8. So the little horn need not arise from a Hellenistic kingdom at all, but can simply come from one of the directions toward which Alexander's kingdom was divided. This agrees with our previous conclusion that the little horn in Daniel 7 is a Roman power.

2. In Daniel 8, the Medo-Persian ram "magnified himself" (verse 4), Alexander's Greek goat "magnified himself exceedingly" (verse 8), and the little horn "grew exceedingly great" (verse 9). Antiochus never achieved a "greatness" comparable to that of Alexander the Great or even Media-Persia.

3. The earthly powers in Daniel 8 replace each other: Media-Persia gives way to Alexander's united Greek kingdom, which, in turn, divides into the four Greek kingdoms, and they yield to the little horn which is presented as a separate empire. Antiochus did not replace

another kingdom in this way. Rather, he was simply part of one of the four Greek kingdoms.

Where is imperial Rome?

Now we are stuck with a dilemma. In Daniel 7, the Roman Church little horn arose from the imperial Roman monster, but Daniel 8 moves directly from the four Hellenistic kingdoms to the little horn. Where is imperial Rome in this chapter? There are two options. Either this vision simply skips over imperial Rome, or the little horn includes imperial Rome. The latter option seems to work best because verse 9 has the little horn expanding in three *horizontal* directions, corresponding to the directions of imperial Rome's initial expansion. "Verse 9 states that the little horn pushed its conquests 'to the south and to the east and toward the Beautiful Land.' These directions fit Rome perfectly as it picked off the four main pieces of the Greek Empire—Macedonia and Pergamum to the east in 168 and 133 B.C., the 'Beautiful Land' of Judea in 60 B.C., and Egypt to the south in 33 B.C."[1] Then verses 10–12 describe the horn's *vertical* thrusts up against heaven, implying that it has become transformed into a religious power.[2]

Why would Daniel 8 combine imperial and papal Rome under the same symbol? Perhaps in order to emphasize the continuity between them, which is even greater than in Daniel 7, where the little horn (Church of Rome), which is different from the earlier horns, sprouts from the fourth beast (imperial Rome), which is "different" from the earlier beasts (verses 7, 23, 24).[3] Notice the similarity here between the fourth beast and the little horn: They are both different.

Another possibility is that Daniel 8 avoids a separate, third animal for imperial Rome because it wants to limit the vision to two animals—ram and he-goat—that have significance as a pair. Unlike the carnivorous beasts in Daniel 7, these are domestic animals. In fact, they are sacrificial animals.

To be more precise, this combination of animals is found in only one ancient Israelite ritual context—as the two sacrifices of the Israelite nonpriestly community in the solemn ceremonies of the Day of Atonement (Leviticus 16:5, 15, 24).[4] The order of animals in Daniel

8 (ram and then goat) reverses that of Leviticus 16 (goat and then ram). Such reversal (today often called "chiasm") was a common Hebrew way to unify a literary unit (for example, Genesis 2:4: "the heavens and the earth . . . earth and heaven") or link one passage to another. We find linkage by reversal even between elements that cross over from the Old Testament to the New Testament. In Leviticus' presentation of sacrifices we read about the blood of an animal and then the body, but at the Last Supper, Christ instituted bread and wine as symbols of His sacrificed body and then blood (Matthew 26:26–28). Another example is the phrase "a festival or a new moon or a Sabbath day" (Colossians 2:16), which reverses and refers back to Numbers 28 and 29, where the order is Sabbath, new moon, and (annual) festivals.

Daniel 8 contains other striking connections to the Israelite sanctuary/temple system and the Day of Atonement:

1. In verse 11, the little horn removes the *tamid,* the "regular/continual" (the so-called "daily")—that is, regular worship. The Hebrew word *tamid,* "regularity/regular," qualifies a cluster of regular worship activities performed at the Israelite sanctuary, including weekly renewal of the "bread of the Presence" (Exodus 25:30; Leviticus 24:8), daily maintenance of the lamps on the lamp stand so that they could burn nightly (Exodus 27:20; Leviticus 24:2–4), daily/continual mediation by the high priest, as represented by his unique garments (Exodus 28:29, 30, 38), the daily burnt offering (Exodus 29:38, 42), daily burning of incense (Exodus 30:8), regular/continual maintenance of fire on the outer altar (Leviticus 6:13), and the high priest's regular grain offering (Leviticus 6:20).

2. In Daniel 8:11, the place of God's sanctuary is thrown down (see also verse 13).

3. Daniel 8:12 refers to rebellion/transgression against the regular worship of God. The word for rebellion here is a form of *pesha*, which appears in pentateuchal ritual law only in the context of the Day of Atonement (Leviticus 16:16, 21).

4. In Daniel 8:14, God's sanctuary is restored through being "justified/vindicated."

So there is a three-step progression: from (1) "regular" worship of God to (2) problems caused by rebellion against Him, followed by (3) restoration of His sanctuary, which represents His reputation

39

and authority. This progression parallels that of the ancient Israelite religious year: (1) Regular ritual services—including sacrifices, burning incense, and so on—were performed throughout the year. (2) Those who were disloyal to God could defile His sanctuary by neglecting His provisions to remedy their faultiness (Numbers 19:13, 20) or by engaging in alternate systems of worship that were opposed to God (Leviticus 20:3). (3) However, at the end of the year, on the Day of Atonement, the sanctuary would be cleansed, signifying that God's reputation would be justified/vindicated (Leviticus 16).

Justifying God's sanctuary through a judgment?

Now we arrive at our central question regarding Daniel 8: What is the relationship between the cleansing/justifying of the sanctuary in this chapter and the pre-Advent judgment in Daniel 7? In Daniel 8:13, the question to which verse 14 responds, it is clear that justifying the sanctuary solves the religious problems created by the little-horn power, just as in chapter 7 the judgment remedies the problem of the little horn. So in some sense, the two events—judgment and justifying the sanctuary—are really one event because they are functionally equivalent, just as the terms "Christmas," "Noel," and "Yuletide," may emphasize slightly different aspects but name the same event.

How could a judgment justify God's sanctuary?

God's sanctuary represents His reputation, character, and authority. It's the headquarters of His administration, where He has His throne (Jeremiah 17:12). So, the sanctuary is like "the White House," which may refer to the current U.S. presidency, not simply a building on Pennsylvania Avenue in Washington, D.C. The idea that God's sanctuary represents His reputation is confirmed by the fact that His "name" was present at the sanctuary (Deuteronomy 12:5, 11), and His name has to do with His reputation (Ezekiel 20:9), just as a good or bad name in human business or politics refers to a positive or negative reputation.

The common denominator of the judgment and the justification of the sanctuary is God's reputation. As we have already found, the judgment justifies/vindicates God's reputation, which is represented by His sanctuary! "In view of the idea of vindication in 8:14 and the fact that 'Son of man' in the preceding chapter also represents vindication—the promises regarding the kingdom of God couched in the imagery of a new (cleansed, restored, vindicated) temple—it is not strange that some scholars have seen that 8:14 symbolically presents the same judgment pictured in 7:9–13."[5]

The Day of Atonement connection confirms the connection between sanctuary and judgment: This day of cleansing the sanctuary was Israel's judgment day, when the loyal were affirmed (Leviticus 16:30) and the disloyal were condemned (Leviticus 23:29, 30).[6] So in Daniel 7 and 8, the solution to the problem of the little horn, including its effect on God and on His people, is an awesome event that functions as a great, end-time Day of Atonement before Jesus comes to earth again.

Some object to the idea of a pre-Advent investigative or demonstrative judgment on the grounds that such an event would deny the forgiveness that we've already received in Christ. But the Israelite Day of Atonement didn't deal with forgiveness all over again, as if forgiveness gained through sacrifices during the year were suddenly rendered null and void. In fact, against almost universal scholarly misconception for two thousand years, the biblical passages regarding the Day of Atonement (Leviticus 16; 23:26–32; Numbers 29:7–11) say nothing at all about forgiveness. Atonement, yes, but not forgiveness.

The "atonement" of the Day of Atonement is a moral cleansing that is a stage of atonement beyond forgiveness (Leviticus 16:30). It builds on the level of reconciliation with God that is already accomplished and goes even further, just as a master's degree builds on a bachelor's degree rather than doing it all over again.

Rather than removing their assurance, the judgment reaffirms it.

In the ancient sanctuary, when the high priest enacted the judgment on the Day of Atonement, he didn't cleanse the sanctuary by wiping off the bloodstains that had been applied for sins during the year. No, he put more blood in several of the same places (Leviticus 16:14-19; compare 4:6, 7, 17, 18, 25, 30, 34), reaffirming the forgiveness that had already been given.

Whose blood did that represent? Christ's blood! Christ's sacrifice is so great that it not only purchases our forgiveness, it pays the cost of mercy after forgiveness, thereby reaffirming our atonement, our reconciliation with God. Let's hear it again for the blood of Christ!

Christ's blood applied to you in the judgment says: You are really forgiven and finally cleansed from any impediments to your covenant relationship with God. You belong to God, not to Satan.[7]

Some sincere, committed, and well-meaning Adventists teach that God's holy people vindicate Him in the judgment by living in obedience to His commandments so that Satan's charge that God's law cannot be kept is shown to be false. There is some truth here, but the emphasis is misplaced on what human beings do for God. It is more biblically accurate to say that God vindicates Himself by what He does for, in, and by those people who accept the gifts that He has lavished on us through Christ. All repentance, forgiveness, and power for holy living comes from Him, so to Him goes all the glory!

Just as Daniel 7 places a time limit on the persecutions of the little horn (verse 25, "a time, times, and half a time"), Daniel 8 limits the time during which God's sanctuary would suffer defilement: "Unto 2,300 evenings-mornings,* then the sanctuary shall be justified" (my translation). In a later chapter of the present book we will pursue details of these periods, but for now it is enough to consider their overall implications: Evil that opposes God and oppresses His people will not go on forever. God is in control of human affairs, even knowing them in advance, and He sets the big deadlines. His salvation is not just a nebulous, spiritual abstraction, but reaches into our history, which is measured by historical time. He is the God both of time and of eternity.

Parallel historical outlines

Thus far we have studied Daniel 2, 7, and 8 and have found clear parallels between the historical outlines of these prophecies, which

---

*Literally, "evening-morning," but in Hebrew, the singular form is used with large numbers—so the meaning is "evenings-mornings."

reach from Daniel's time to the end of the present era. There are also parallels in the Babylonian "Dynastic Prophecy," which begins with Assyria and moves through Babylon and then Persia (one empire, not Medes and Persians) to the Macedonians/Greeks.[8] Furthermore, the New Testament descriptions of the coming "lawless one" in 2 Thessalonians 2 and the "beast" in the book of Revelation (especially chapters 13; 19) obviously correspond to the depictions of the little-horn power in Daniel. Both of these passages note this entity's opposition to God and His law and its final destruction by Him at Christ's second coming.

Revelation 11 alludes to the judgment/justifying of the sanctuary, thereby combining the events in Daniel 7 and 8: "The seventh angel sounded; and there arose loud voices in heaven, saying, 'The kingdom of the world has become the kingdom of our Lord, and of His Christ; and He will reign forever and ever. . . . And the nations were enraged, and Thy wrath came, and the time came for the dead to be judged, and the time to give their reward to Thy bond-servants the prophets and to the saints and to those who fear Thy name, the small and the great, and to destroy those who destroy the earth.' And the temple of God which is in heaven was opened; and the ark of His covenant appeared in His temple" (verses 15, 18, 19). The fact that the ark appears implies a strong connection with the Day of Atonement, which was the only time when anyone (the high priest) was permitted to open and enter the Holy of Holies, where the ark was located (Leviticus 16).

We can outline the parallel presentations of the sequence of events from Old Testament times to the end of human rule on planet Earth found in Daniel, the "Dynastic Prophecy," and the New Testament, as follows. (Explicit identifications of human powers in the various texts are shown in italics.)

These parallels give us the overwhelming impression that the historical progression from Babylon to the destruction of earthly powers is sure and important. They also show that the judgment and the justification of the sanctuary occur in the same relative time slot, which confirms that they really are the same event.

The timing of this event is late in human history, after the little horn/Church of Rome has done its work for some time. Since the Church of Rome was not established in any sense until after the

Daniel 2	Daniel 7	Daniel 8	Dynastic Prophecy	New Testament
			Assyria	
Gold Babylon	Lion		Babylon	
Silver	Bear	Ram Media-Persia	Persia	
Bronze	Leopard	Goat Greece	Macedonia (Greece)	
Iron	Monster	Horn (horizontal)		Imperial Rome
	Horn	Horn (vertical)		"lawless one" or "beast"
	judgment	justifying sanctuary		
destruction of earthly powers	destruction of earthly powers	destruction of earthly powers		destruction of earthly powers

Second Temple (Herod's temple) was destroyed in Jerusalem in A.D. 70, the sanctuary that is justified in Daniel 8:14 cannot be the earthly temple, which no longer exists. It must be God's heavenly temple, which is referred to in various places in the Bible (for example, Psalm 11:4) and the function of which is described in the book of Hebrews (especially chapters 7–10). In the end time, the worldwide Day of Atonement judgment is not convened at an earthly temple of localized significance. Rather, it meets in God's heavenly temple, the control center of the entire universe, where no human powers or any evil in-

44

fluence can interfere with the proceedings. This is good news for God's people, who receive the benefit of a judgment that is completely fair because God controls it (see Psalm 96).

1. William H. Shea, Daniel 7–12: *Prophecies of the End Time,* The Abundant Life Bible Amplifier (Nampa, Idaho: Pacific Press®, 1996), 39.

2. William H. Shea, "Spatial Dimensions in the Vision of Daniel 8," *Symposium on Daniel,* Daniel and Revelation Committee Series 2, Frank H. Holbrook, ed. (Silver Spring, Md.: Biblical Research Institute, 1986), 507–526. Alberto Treiyer concludes "that only the geographical projections of this horn, or power, needed be identified more specifically with the heathen Roman empire (v. 9), to allow us to determine more easily the throne and the place of the Christian empire that would succeed the former empire in the same city and territory (cf. Rev 13:2-3)." *The Day of Atonement and the Heavenly Judgment From the Pentateuch to Revelation* (Siloam Springs, Ark.: Creation Enterprises International, 1992), 338, 339.

3. John T. Anderson, *Investigating the Judgment* (Hagerstown, Md.: Review and Herald, 2003), 37–39.

4. Jacques Doukhan, Daniel: *The Vision of the End,* rev. ed. (Berrien Springs, Mich.: Andrews University Press, 1987), 26–29.

5. Desmond Ford, *Daniel* (Nashville: Southern Publishing Association, 1978), 163.

6. Compare the way Jews still observe Yom Kippur, the Day of Atonement, as a day of judgment according to rabbinic tradition. See Jacques Doukhan, *Secrets of Daniel: Wisdom and Dreams of a Jewish Prince in Exile* (Hagerstown, Md.: Review and Herald, 2000), 128, 129; Roy Gane, *Cult and Character: Purification Offerings, Day of Atonement, and Theodicy* (Winona Lake, Ind.: Eisenbrauns, 2005), 307–309.

7. Roy Gane, *Altar Call* (Berrien Springs, Mich.: Diadem, 1999), 340. The fulfillment of the typology/symbolism of the Day of Atonement began at the Cross because that is when Christ's sacrificial blood was shed. But the fact that the writer of Hebrews 10 considered the judgment still to be future shows that the application of Christ's blood *for the purpose of cleansing God's sanctuary/judgment* did not begin until some time after the Crucifixion. Notice also that Hebrews 10:28 mentions the testimony of witnesses, implying investigative judgment.

8. A. K. Grayson, *Babylonian Historical-Literary Texts* (Toronto: University of Toronto Press, 1975), 24–37.

CHAPTER 6

The Fate of God's Temple, City, and People

(Daniel 9:1-23)

The visions of Daniel 7 and 8 predict a succession of human powers culminating in a religious "little horn." After a judgment that vindicates God's character as He affirms the loyal but condemns the disloyal, His eternal kingdom replaces that of the little horn. Although explanations accompanied both of the visions of Daniel 7 and 8, they deeply disturbed the prophet. The end of chapter 8 says that he didn't understand the vision recorded in that chapter, so at least in that case, the explanation he received was incomplete. A big link (not a Little Link!) was missing.

We find it highly frustrating when part of a story, picture, or pattern is missing. It is said that when Mozart was a boy, on the days when he didn't want to get out of bed in the morning one of his family members would play a scale on the piano but stop just before the last note. Little Wolfgang couldn't stand having the scale unfinished, so he would leap out of bed and run to the piano to play the final note!

The stakes of completion were much higher for Daniel than for Mozart. For Daniel, "the rest of the story" is recorded in chapter 9 of his book. Daniel 9 begins like this: "In the first year of Darius the son of Ahasuerus, of Median descent, who was made king over the kingdom of the Chaldeans—in the first year of his reign I, Daniel, observed in the books the number of the years which was revealed as the word of the LORD to Jeremiah the prophet for the completion of the desolations of Jerusalem, namely, seventy years. So I gave my attention to the Lord God to seek Him by prayer and supplications, with fasting, sackcloth, and ashes" (verses 1–3).

Why would the prophecy of Jeremiah be of special interest to Daniel at this time? Regarding the country of Judah, the Lord had predicted through Jeremiah: " ' "This whole land shall be a desolation and a horror, and these nations shall serve the king of Babylon seventy years. Then it will be when seventy years are completed I will punish the king of Babylon and that nation," declares the LORD, "for their iniquity, and the land of the Chaldeans; and I will make it an everlasting desolation" ' " (Jeremiah 25:11, 12). " 'Thus says the LORD, "When seventy years have been completed for Babylon, I will visit you and fulfill My good word to you, to bring you back to this place" ' " (Jeremiah 29:10).

So at the end of seventy years of oppression by Babylon, when that empire would be punished, the Jewish people would be free to go home. Daniel, who was now an old man and knew that the seventy years were reaching their expiration date, should have considered this good news. So why was he upset, as shown by his fasting with sackcloth and ashes?

Notice the date in Daniel 9:1: "the first year of Darius." The content of this chapter dates to the beginning not merely of a new king's reign but of a new empire: Media-Persia, the second of the four kingdoms of Daniel 2 and 7. Again, this should have been good news. When Media-Persia had conquered Babylon, thereby fulfilling the prophecy of Jeremiah, it should have been about time for the exiled Jews to return home.[1] But the fact that Daniel was deeply distressed implies that he knew something else. What could it have been?

The problem was that just a few years before, he had learned in the vision recorded in chapter 8 of his book that God's sanctuary would be justified only after "2,300 evenings-mornings," during which time a series of empires would rise and fall and an evil religious power would oppose God and His people. The prior vision of Daniel 7 confirmed the sequence of empires and the role of the evil religious power; what made Daniel 8 so distressing was the status of the sanctuary during the 2,300 evenings-mornings.

47

Not having the New Testament books of Hebrews and Revelation, Daniel would most naturally assume that the sanctuary was the temple in Jerusalem. The Babylonians had destroyed Solomon's temple when they had destroyed Jerusalem and exiled its inhabitants. So Daniel would link the temple, city, and people in his understanding of the vision of Daniel 8. He thought this vision meant that his people would be required to wait an additional 2,300 difficult evenings-mornings before they could return home and rebuild their city and God's temple.

If Daniel had interpreted the 2,300 evenings-mornings as literal twenty-four-hour days, he wouldn't have been so upset. When you've waited seventy years, six-and-a-third more years isn't a long delay. But clearly, the prophet didn't take the 2,300 evenings-mornings to be literal days. He knew that during this time several mighty empires would rise and fall. This would take much longer than six-plus years. So the delay would be huge.

Comparing God's promise through Jeremiah with the additional revelation Daniel himself had received, he would have wondered why there was a discrepancy of such biblical proportions. Had God intended all along that the restoration of the temple, city, and people should be delayed for more than two thousand years after Babylon fell, or had the sins of the Jews brought additional punishment upon them? Daniel knew that in either case the cause of their plight was their sinful disloyalty to God and His covenant.

Daniel's prayer

The bulk of Daniel 9 (verses 4–19) consists of the prayer Daniel offered on this occasion. It is one of the most beautiful and powerful prayers preserved in the Bible. Although Daniel was confessing sins and seeking God's mercy, the fact that he did this not only on behalf of himself but also on behalf of his people means that his prayer was one of intercession. Compare Ezekiel 14:14, 20, where Daniel is known to Ezekiel, his contemporary, as a great intercessor. As an effective mediator with God, Daniel identified himself with his people, using the pronoun "we" rather than "they": " 'We have sinned, committed iniquity, acted wickedly and rebelled, even turning aside from Your commandments and ordinances' " (Daniel 9:5, NAU, emphasis supplied).

The Fate of God's Temple, City, and People (Daniel 9:1-23)

It isn't surprising that Daniel's prayer focuses on his concern for Jerusalem, its temple, and his people, who had suffered the covenant curses because of rebellion against God. The basis of his appeal for mercy was God's own character. He began his prayer: " 'Alas, O Lord, the great and awesome God, who keeps His covenant and lovingkindness for those who love Him and keep His commandments' " (verse 4, NAU). These words echo the description God gave Moses of His own character (see Exodus 34:6, 7; see also Exodus 20:5, 6). When the Israelites sinned at Kadesh by faithlessly refusing to take the Promised Land as Caleb and Joshua urged them to do, Moses interceded by citing God's character and appealing to His desire to preserve His reputation in the world (Numbers 14:13–19).

Following Moses' lead, Daniel ended his prayer by appealing to God's merciful character and the concern He should have for the city and people who are called by His name and thus are linked to His reputation: " 'O my God, incline Your ear and hear! Open Your eyes and see our desolations and the city which is called by Your name; for we are not presenting our supplications before You on account of any merits of our own, but on account of Your great compassion. O Lord, hear! O Lord, forgive! O Lord, listen and take action! For Your own sake, O my God, do not delay, because Your city and Your people are called by Your name' " (Daniel 9:18, 19, NAU).

Numbers 14 reports that God directly answered Moses' prayer, saying that He pardoned the Israelite people in the sense of allowing their nation to continue (verses 20–37). God's answer to Daniel was just as prompt, but He answered through His messenger, Gabriel. At least on the surface, what Gabriel said had to do primarily with explanation rather than forgiveness (Daniel 9:20–27). However, the words of the angel, " 'for you are highly esteemed' " (verse 23, NAU), show that God accepted Daniel and his prayer for mercy and forgiveness.

Gabriel went on to say, " 'Give heed to the message and gain understanding of the vision' " (verse 23, NAU). What vision? There is no vision in Daniel 9! Gabriel must be referring to the previous vision—that of Daniel 8, which specifically dealt with God's sanctuary and people, the central concerns of Daniel's prayer in chapter 9 (see verse

20). In our next chapter, we will investigate Gabriel's explanation in Daniel 9:24–27, which pinpoints the identity of the Messiah with startling exactness and reveals the sacrificial basis of God's forgiveness and restoration of Israel, for which Daniel prayed. Through Christ's sacrifice, God would indeed preserve His reputation for justice and mercy.

---

1. For the interpretation that the seventy years of Babylonian exile lasted from the first deportation of the Jews to Babylonia in the Jewish fall-to-fall civil year 606/605 B.C. until the return of a large group of exiles in about 537/536 B.C. (with Jewish inclusive reckoning, which counted the portions of the beginning and ending years as though they were full years), see *The Seventh-Day Adventist Bible Commentary*, Francis D. Nichol, ed. (Hagerstown, Md.: Review and Herald, 1954), 3:90–92, 94–97.

CHAPTER

7

Ultimate Atonement Through the Messiah!
(Daniel 9:24-27)

We have found that in Daniel 9, Gabriel came to Daniel to help him understand the vision recorded in Daniel 8, which reached from the Medo-Persian period until the end time. In light of the prediction that a series of human powers would rise and fall during "2,300 evenings-mornings" before God's sanctuary would be "justified" (8:14), Daniel's big concern was the fate of the temple, Jerusalem, and the Jewish people. Would they continue to be desolate for a long time while God's enemies ground them down? If so, how would Jeremiah's prophecy of restoration after seventy years of Babylonian oppression (25:11, 12; 29:10) be fulfilled?

Daniel's main questions had to do with the fate of the temple, Jerusalem, and the Jews during the immediate future, beginning with the period of domination by Media-Persia. So, Gabriel answered by explaining what would happen during this time (Daniel 9:24–27). Yes, the prophecy of Jeremiah would be fulfilled in the short-term; the Jewish people would soon be restored to Jerusalem and the temple would be rebuilt. But there would be more to the story. The time of the second temple would be troubled; the Jews would experience desolation, abominations, and the eventual destruction of this temple.

In his prayer, Daniel had acknowledged that the sins of his people had broken their covenant with God and brought the curses of the covenant (Leviticus 26; Deuteronomy 28) down upon them. So it would not be enough for them to go back to their Promised Land. If they kept rebelling against God, they would bring more destruction and exile upon themselves in the future. Lasting restoration and the ultimate fulfillment of God's plan for His people, as revealed through visions and other prophetic revelations, required a permanent solution to the problem of their sins. It required eternal righteousness. God Himself would provide this solution during a period of "seventy weeks": "Seventy weeks have been cut off (or 'determined') concerning your people and concerning your holy city to finish the transgression (or 'rebellious sin'), and to stop sins, and to atone for iniquity (or 'culpability'), and to bring eternal righteousness, and to seal vision and prophet, and to anoint a holy of holies" (Daniel 9:24, my translation).

This verse, at the beginning of Gabriel's explanation, addresses all three major concerns of Daniel's prayer: "your people," "your holy city" (Jerusalem), and "a holy of holies" (the temple). We have already found that these concerns arose from Daniel's comparison of his own vision of Daniel 8 with Jeremiah's prophecy. We also saw that the Day of Atonement was a prominent theme in Daniel 8. Now we find Day of Atonement language in Daniel 9:24. The three Hebrew terms for moral faults listed here—translated "transgression," "sins," and "iniquity"—also appear together in Leviticus 16. In verses 16, 18, 19, "transgression" (unforgivable rebellious sins) and "sins" (forgivable and forgiven sins) are purged from the three areas of God's sanctuary, beginning with the holy of holies. And in verse 21, "iniquities" (culpabilities), "transgressions," and "sins" are banished on a live goat (the so-called scapegoat) to the wilderness, to a being called Azazel.[1]

The seventy weeks and the jubilee year

The seventy-weeks prophecy contains another important—though less direct—connection to the Day of Atonement. Daniel's seventy weeks following the Babylonian captivity are obviously related to Jeremiah's earlier prophecy of seventy years of exile. Jeremiah's seventy years, in turn, are related to sabbatical years, when agricultural land was supposed to rest (Leviticus 25:1–7). Leviticus 26 cites covenant disobedience by the Israelites as a reason that " ' "the land shall be abandoned by them, and shall make up for its sabbaths while it is made desolate without them" ' " (verse 43). Describing the catastrophe of conquest, destruction, and exile by the Babylonians, 2 Chronicles 36:21 links Leviticus 25 and 26 with Jeremiah when it observes that these events were "to fulfill the word of the LORD by the mouth of Jeremiah, until the land had enjoyed its sabbaths. All the days of its desolation it kept sabbath until seventy years were complete." So the seventy years of national exile included punishment for the failure of Israelite farmers to keep a sabbatical year every seven years.

Having found a clear link between Daniel's seventy weeks and the sabbatical years of Leviticus 25, we can recognize a connection between the seventy weeks and the jubilee year, which begins on the Day of Atonement after seven sabbatical year periods. The jubilee is prescribed in Leviticus 25:8–10: " ' "You are also to count off seven sabbaths of years for yourself, seven times seven years, so that you have the time of the seven sabbaths of years, namely, forty-nine years. You shall then sound a ram's horn abroad on the tenth day of the seventh month; on the day of atonement you shall sound a horn all through your land. You shall thus consecrate the fiftieth year and proclaim a release through the land to all its inhabitants. It shall be a jubilee for you, and each of you shall return to his own property, and each of you shall return to his family." ' "

In this law, time is counted in multiples of seven, based on the concept of the seventh-day Sabbath (*Sabbath* means "rest"/ "cessation"), when there was to be rest from work (Exodus 20:8–11). But in Leviticus 25:8–10, "sabbaths" are explicitly "of years" rather than days. Compare the sabbatical year in Exodus 23:10, 11, paralleling the Sabbath day in verse 12. So these "sabbaths of years" divide time into weeks of years, that is, sabbatical year cycles.[2] After seven times seven years—in other words, forty-nine years—there would be a proclamation of freedom, when each impoverished Israelite who had lost his ability to support himself and his family on his own agricultural land would regain his ancestral property and be released from debt servitude. This freedom would be proclaimed by the jubilee trumpet on the Day of Atonement!

Daniel 9:24 speaks of a period of seventy weeks—that is, seventy times seven, or 490 "days." If that were literal days, it would total less than a year and a half—not nearly long enough for the restoration of Jerusalem (verse 25). So the "weeks" must be weeks of years, adding up to 490 years. At the end of this time there was to be a release, not simply from loss of farmland and freedom by individual Israelites ("each of you," Leviticus 25:10) who needed this help, but freedom from sin for the entire nation, which would provide for eternal freedom and security. This, then, would be a greater kind of jubilee. The idea is reinforced by the fact that 490 years can be divided into ten ordinary jubilee periods of forty-nine years each, as confirmed by the inclusion of seven weeks (forty-nine years) at the beginning of the 490 years (Daniel 9:25).

We have found that numbers are associated with themes. Comparing Daniel 9 with Leviticus 25, we find that the greater number of years until the release corresponds to the greater scope of the release:

Reference	Scope of Release	Years
Leviticus 25	each individual	49
Daniel 9	entire nation	490

The allusions to the Day of Atonement in Daniel 8 and 9 contribute to the integral connection between these chapters. In Daniel 8:14, justifying/vindicating God's sanctuary in heaven makes sense in the context of an end-time Day of Atonement judgment. It does so because the Day of Atonement of the ancient Israelites was the time when the purity of the sanctuary, which represented God's character and reputation, was restored and His people were judged according to their loyalty or lack thereof (Leviticus 16; 23:26–32). And what is the function of the connections to the Day of Atonement that we find in Daniel 9:24? This verse contains nothing about justifying or cleansing the sanctuary/temple. Rather, we find the words "to anoint a holy of holies," which have to do with an initial consecration of a sanctuary and its priesthood (see, for example, Exodus 29; Leviticus 8).

This consecration and the Day of Atonement are closely related because the Day of Atonement restores the sanctuary to the state of purity established at its initial consecration. In fact, Leviticus 16:19

says that when the sanctuary is cleansed on the Day of Atonement, its altar is (re)consecrated. So it appears that Daniel 9:24 speaks of the anointing/consecration of the sanctuary that later needs to be "justified" through an end-time Day of Atonement (8:14).

Two temples

Daniel 9:24 outlines permanent, overall goals that God will accomplish by the end of the seventy weeks of years along with bringing in "eternal righteousness." This seems to contradict Daniel 9:26: "The people of the coming leader will destroy the city and the temple" (my translation). If the temple were to be rebuilt during the seventy weeks and subsequently destroyed, how could its consecration have a lasting effect associated with abolishing sin and establishing eternal righteousness?

The answer must be that Daniel 9 speaks of two different temples. One is a temple that takes the place of Solomon's temple, which the Babylonians had destroyed. This second temple would be built in a restored Jerusalem following the exile (verse 25), but later it too would be destroyed (verse 26). Therefore, it wouldn't make a lasting contribution to the eradication of sin and the bringing in of eternal righteousness. These benefits would be accomplished through anointing another temple and priesthood (verse 24) and through confirmation of a divine covenant "with the many" by the Anointed One—that is, the Messiah (verse 27)!

"The 70 weeks have not been 'determined' *against* the Jews to mark their fate or imply the rejection of Israel. The purpose of the 70 weeks is, instead, the good news of the salvation of the Jews and of the world through the work of the new High Priest. This event, which took place in A.D. 31 as reported by Peter, describes Jesus as sitting at the right hand of the Father after His ascension (1 Peter 3:22). Further the event is confirmed in A.D. 34, precisely at the end of the 70 weeks, by Stephen, who saw at that very moment 'the heavens opened and the Son of Man standing at the right hand of God!' (Acts 7:56)."[3]

Just as the ancient Israelite tabernacle and its Aaronic priests were anointed to consecrate them for their function within the context of the divine covenant, another temple and priesthood would be anointed as part of the divine covenant. This time the anointed priest would be the ultimate Anointed One. He is the divine Priest-King of the order of Melchizedek ("King of Righteousness") spoken of by Psalm 110—One who sits at the right hand of God. No wonder this priesthood and temple would be able to dispose of moral faults completely and establish eternal righteousness! This Messiah-Priest would reign forever. Therefore, we are to identify Him with the "One like a Son of Man" in Daniel 7:13, 14.

While the Messiah would accomplish everlasting results, in the short-term, He would be "cut off and have nothing/nobody" (Daniel 9:26, my translation). In other words, He would suffer the divinely administered judicial penalty of "cutting off" (compare, for example, Leviticus 20:3; Numbers 15:30, 31), which was reserved in Old Testament times for rebellious sinners for whom the sacrificial system of the sanctuary/temple made no provision for forgiveness. According to Donald Wold, who wrote his Ph.D. dissertation on the biblical penalty of "cutting off," this punishment meant that the sinner's line of descendants was eventually cut off, thereby denying him/her an afterlife.[4] A person who was "cut off" would have nobody to carry on the memory of his or her name and would be lost to history. This prefigures the eternal cutting off from God that is the second death (Revelation 20).

In Daniel 9:26, the words "and have nothing/nobody" describe the aloneness of the One who is cut off, who in this case is the Messiah. He would die with nobody to help Him (compare Daniel 11:45), crying out, "My God, my God, why have you forsaken me? . . . Be not far from me, for trouble is near; for there is none to help" (Psalm 22:1, 11, NAU).

The fact that the Messiah confirms a covenant "with the many" (Daniel 9:27) reminds us of the role of God's suffering servant: "He shall see the labor of His soul, and be satisfied. By His knowledge My righteous Servant shall justify *many*, for He shall bear their iniquities" (Isaiah 53:11, NKJV, emphasis supplied).

Christ as Sacrifice and High Priest

The links between Daniel 9, Psalm 22, and Isaiah 53 point to the same Messiah (Christ), who is identified in the New Testament as Jesus of Nazareth. He confirmed God's covenant with many by dying for them (including us!), apparently forsaken by God (Matthew 27:46, quoting Psalm 22:1)—the equivalent of the second death. But although Christ died the ultimate death from which there is no return, with no descendants or afterlife, He did arise to "see His [spiritual] offspring" (Isaiah 53:10) because He was really innocent and sacrificed Himself to make intercession for sinners (verses 10–12).

Now we can better understand the words in Daniel 9:27: "He shall make sacrifice and grain offering cease" (my translation)—that is, the Messiah shall put an end to the significance of the sacrificial system at the temple in Jerusalem. When Jesus died, "the veil of the temple was torn in two from top to bottom" (Matthew 27:51), thereby profaning the temple by laying its Most Holy Place open to public view. In terms of providing access to the Most Holy Place, this was like a Day of Atonement. The difference was that previously, only the high priest had this special access (Leviticus 16). Now, Jesus had accomplished the once-for-all sacrifice to which all the animal sacrifices pointed, including the sacrifices of the Day of Atonement and those of the Passover. Because He died, ascended to heaven, and is ministering in God's temple there (Hebrews 7–10), all believers on earth have direct access to God. Through Christ, our divine-human High Priest, we are all like human high priests in the sense that by faith, all of us can approach the throne of God (Hebrews 4:14–16; 6:19, 20; see also Day of Atonement imagery in Hebrews 9).

According to the New Testament, there is no such thing as a *legitimate* earthly Christian priesthood consisting of elite human ministers who mediate for their people before God by performing rituals and other activities. The apostle Paul taught, "There is one God, and one mediator also between God and men, the man Christ Jesus" (1 Timothy 2:5). Peter said of all Christians: "You are a chosen race, a royal priesthood, a holy nation, a people for God's own possession, that you may proclaim the excellencies of Him who has called you out of darkness into His marvelous light" (1 Peter 2:9). "According to Peter, all Christians belong to the priesthood. In the New Testament, the church does not *have* a priesthood—it *is* a priesthood."[5]

A "Christian" religious system that has an elite, exclusive human priesthood implicitly denies that Christ's once-for-all atoning sacrifice has achieved its goal of giving all believers equal access directly to God through the heavenly ministry of our one High Priest, Jesus Christ. Such a system commits blasphemy by usurping the role of

57

the divine Christ. It is idolatrous in the sense that it illegitimately directs people's faith to earthly things, as if these could help them find divine favor the way the Israelites thought the golden calf could benefit them (Exodus 32).

Is there a "Christian priesthood" today?

Yes, in several denominations, including the Church of Rome and other churches influenced by it.

Is this kind of human "priesthood" legitimate?

Not according to the Bible. It denies Christ and is blasphemous. In fact, in the Roman Mass, "they again crucify to themselves the Son of God, and put Him to open shame" (Hebrews 6:6). So, is it any wonder that the Bible has profiled the Church of Rome as the little-horn power of Daniel 7 and 8?

Is the point of view expressed here "politically correct"? To the contrary—but who says the Bible is "politically correct"? Postmodern, pluralistic philosophy that accepts everything as valid and legitimate if it "works for you" contradicts the Bible, which says that there is salvation only in Christ (Acts 4:12). However, if we are to be free to practice our religion, we must grant the same freedom to others. Even if we do not accept their choices, we must respect their right to choose. I am grateful for the freedom of expression we enjoy while we have separation of church and state. In another time and/ or place, I could have been killed for what I am writing here.

---

1. Roy Gane, *Leviticus, Numbers,* New International Version Application Commentary (Grand Rapids, Mich.: Zondervan, 2004), 280–283. For more detail, see Roy Gane, *Cult and Character: Purification Offerings, Day of Atonement, and Theodicy* (Winona Lake, Ind.: Eisenbrauns, 2005), 285–302.

2. Jewish scholarship agrees: see Ben Zion Wacholder, "Chronomessianism: The Timing of Messianic Movements and the Calendar of Sabbatical Cycles," *Hebrew Union College Annual* 46 (1975): 202–204; Hersh Goldwurm, *Daniel: A New Translation With a Commentary Anthologized From Talmudic, Midrashic, and Rabbinic Sources* (New York: Mesorah, 1979), 259.

3. Jacques Doukhan, *The Mystery of Israel* (Hagerstown, Md.: Review and Herald, 2004), 36.

4. Donald Wold, "The Meaning of the Biblical Penalty *Kareth*" (Ph.D. dissertation, University of California at Berkeley, 1978).

5. Russell Burrill, *Revolution in the Church* (Fallbrook, Calif.: Hart Research Center, 1979), 24; see also Roy Gane, *Leviticus, Numbers,* NIV Application Commentary (Grand Rapids: Zondervan, 2004), 170–172.

When Does the Pre-Advent Judgment Begin?
(Daniel 8; 9)

Thus far we have learned from the book of Daniel that God vindicates His character, represented by His sanctuary, through an awesome investigative/demonstrative judgment in heaven before Jesus comes to set up God's eternal kingdom on earth (Daniel 7:9–14; 8:14). This judgment occurs after "a time, times, and half a time" of persecution by the little horn power (7:25) and at the end of 2,300 evenings-mornings (8:14). These indicators of time suggest that God wants His people to know at least in relative terms when His judgment begins.

Since the pre-Advent judgment is the last great event before Christ's second coming, it would be helpful for us to know whether it is in the past, present, or future in relation to our time. On the ancient Israelites' Day of Atonement, God expected all of His faithful people to demonstrate their loyalty in a special way by humbling themselves through self-denial and by abstaining from work while His sanctuary was being cleansed (Leviticus 16:29–31; 23:26–32). So, if the end-time judgment is a greater equivalent of the Israelite Day of Atonement, shouldn't Christians know when it begins? If you invite people to an event but your announcement doesn't specify the time, how many people could you expect to show up?

Speaking of the end-time judgment, Revelation 14 proclaims God's special message for this time:

> And I saw another angel flying in midheaven, having an

59

eternal gospel to preach to those who live on the earth, and to every nation and tribe and tongue and people; and he said with a loud voice, "Fear God, and give Him glory, because *the hour of His judgment has come;* and worship Him who made the heaven and the earth and sea and springs of waters." And another angel, a second one, followed, saying, "Fallen, fallen is Babylon the great, she who has made all the nations drink of the wine of the passion of her immorality." And another angel, a third one, followed them, saying with a loud voice, "If anyone worships the beast and his image, and receives a mark on his forehead or upon his hand, he also will drink of the wine of the wrath of God, which is mixed in full strength in the cup of His anger; and he will be tormented with fire and brimstone in the presence of the holy angels and in the presence of the Lamb. And the smoke of their torment goes up forever and ever; and they have no rest day and night, those who worship the beast and his image, and whoever receives the mark of his name." Here is the perseverance of the saints who keep the commandments of God and their faith in Jesus (verses 6–12, emphasis supplied).

The messages of these three angels ("messengers") specifically target people living during the time when God's judgment "has come" (verse 7). The message is "an eternal gospel" (verse 6)—that is, everlasting good news—because it is a culminating part of God's vast plan to save all those who accept Him by faith in Jesus Christ. It contains a powerful warning against idolatrous power that is opposed to God. The previous chapter describes a blasphemous "beast" in terms that identify it with Daniel's little-horn power, which is condemned in God's pre-Advent judgment. So Revelation 14 is talking about the same judgment as that described in Daniel 7 and 8!

With the third-angel's message, Revelation 14:12 characterizes God's loyal ones as those who keep two things during the end-time judgment: (1) the commandments of God and (2) their faith in Jesus. Since this judgment is the ultimate Day of Atonement, it is clear that these two requirements are the functional equivalents of what the ancient Israelites were to do in order to participate in their Day of Atonement: (1) humble themselves before God through physical self-denial, including fasting, and (2) keep Sabbath by abstaining from all work, as on the weekly Sabbath (Leviticus 16:29, 31; 23:27–32).

There are thematic connections between what the ancient Israelites were to do and what end-time Christians are to do. As the Israelites were to humble themselves, end-time Christians are to keep faith in Jesus, who "humbled Himself by becoming obedient to the point of death, even death on a cross" (Philippians 2:8). As the Israelites were to keep Sabbath, end-time Christians are to keep God's commandments, which include the seventh-day Sabbath (Exodus 20:8–11; Deuteronomy 5:12–15).

Exodus 31:13 reveals a more comprehensive link between the Sabbath and God's commandments. Keeping God's Sabbaths is " 'a sign between Me and you throughout your generations, that you may know that I am the LORD who sanctifies you.' " Within the context of the covenant with God, sanctification (becoming holy) means becoming like Him in character (Leviticus 11:44, 45; 19:2; 1 Peter 1:14–16), and His character is love (1 John 4:8), which is the basis of all His commandments (Matthew 22:37–40). So the holy Sabbath celebrates the way God gives us the gift of obedience to His holy law by making us holy through pouring His holy love into our hearts by His Holy Spirit (Romans 5:5)!

It is crystal clear by now that Christians really need to know when the judgment has arrived so that they can intelligently and meaningfully participate in this great event—and so that they can tell others about it in order that they too will have the opportunity to show loyalty to God rather than to the beast/little horn and its allies.

Does the Bible provide enough information for us to find out when the pre-Advent judgment begins? Daniel 7 speaks of three and one half "times" of persecution by the little horn (Daniel 7:25), which come before the judgment delivers God's people from oppression. Since we have found that the little horn represents the Church of Rome, we can gain perspective by learning more about this period (see chapter 9). But more helpful than this is Daniel 8:14, which pinpoints the time when God's sanctuary is "justified," the same event as the judgment in Daniel 7:9–14.

Daniel 8:14 says the judgment comes after the 2,300 evenings-mornings. The problem is that Daniel 8 doesn't give a beginning point for this period, so we don't know when it ends. However, the explanation in Daniel 9 *does* provide a starting point for the seventy weeks/490 years, and this period covers the first segment of the 2,300 evenings-mornings. It is the integral relationship between the vision of Daniel 8 and the explanation in 9:24–27 that combines the two periods and thereby provides the starting point for the 2,300 evenings-mornings.

1844 in ten steps[1]

Now let's look at the ten steps necessary for finding when the pre-Advent, Day of Atonement judgment begins. I'll list them all and then discuss each one more fully. Much of this will be review, but we will need to add some information to fill in some gaps.

Step 1: Identify the little horn (Daniel 8).

Step 2: Recognize that the 2,300 days cannot be literal days.

Step 3: Recognize that Daniel 9 explains the vision of Daniel 8.

Step 4: Identify the date when the seventy weeks (490 days) began.

Step 5: Recognize that the seventy weeks are weeks of years and thus 490 years.

Step 6: Find the end of the 490 years.

Step 7: Recognize that the end of Daniel 9 refers to events that would happen after the 490 years, but still during the 2,300 days.

Step 8: Recognize that the 2,300 days, like the 490 days, must represent years.

Step 9: See how the 490 years overlap the first part of the 2,300 years.

Step 10: Find the end of the 2,300 years.

Step 1: Identify the little horn (Daniel 8)

In Daniel 8, God's sanctuary is justified at the end of "2,300 evenings and mornings" (verse 14) and solves problems caused by an evil little-horn power. The little horn had arisen after a succession of other powers:

- A ram (verses 3, 4) representing the Medo-Persian Empire (verse 20) was conquered by a goat with a big horn (verses 5–7), symbolizing Greece/Macedonia under its first king (verse 21). This must be Alexander the Great, who conquered Media-Persia in the fourth century B.C.

- When Alexander died, his kingdom was split into four Greek kingdoms, represented by four horns in verses 8, 22. The four kingdoms were Ptolemaic Egypt, Seleucid Syria, Attalid Pergamum, and Antigonid Macedonia.
- The little horn arose at the end of the rule of the four kingdoms (verse 23) from one of the four "winds of heaven"—that is, the four directions to which Alexander's empire was divided (verses 8, 9). This little horn built a great empire (verse 9). It was distinct from the four Greek kingdoms and superseded them. Only one power fits this description: Rome. The Roman Empire was in control from shortly before the beginning of the Christian era to the fifth century A.D. The church of Rome superseded the empire, dominating the Middle Ages. If the justifying of God's sanctuary happens after domination by the little horn and if the little horn represents Rome, the sanctuary must be justified after Rome's domination.

Media-Persia ➪ Greece ➪ Four kingdoms ➪ Rome ➪ Sanctuary justified

---

Step 2: Recognize that the 2,300 days cannot be literal days

The question in Daniel 8:13 is: " 'How long is the vision?' " The answer is: " 'For 2,300 evenings and mornings' "—that is, 2,300 days (verse 14). But the vision lasts from the time of the Medo-Persian Empire at the beginning of Daniel 8 (verses 1, 2) until the end of the Roman Empire, a period covering many centuries. This is many times longer than 2,300 literal days, which is less than six-and-a-half years.

Step 3: Recognize that Daniel 9 explains the vision of Daniel 8

Daniel prayed to God (Daniel 9:3–19), who sent Gabriel (verses 20–23) to help him "understand the vision" (verse 23) by giving him additional information. There is no vision in Daniel 9, so the vision referred to must be that of Daniel 8. Gabriel comforted Daniel by telling him that the Jews would be restored to their land and temple sooner than the end of the 2,300 days. Within "seventy weeks," Jerusalem would be restored and "an anointed one," the Messiah, would come (Daniel 9:24–27, NRSV).

Step 4: Identify the date when the seventy weeks (490 days) began

Daniel 9:25 gives the beginning of the seventy weeks: " 'From the issuing of a decree to restore and rebuild Jerusalem.' " The decree that resulted in the restoration of Jerusalem as the capital of the Jews was that of the Persian king Artaxerxes. It was made in the seventh year of his reign (Ezra 7), which was 457 B.C.[2]

Step 5: Recognize that the seventy weeks are weeks of years and thus 490 years

The seventy weeks began during the Persian era and were to include the rebuilding of Jerusalem and the coming of the Messiah. How could all that happen in seventy weeks of literal days—that is, 490 days?

Leviticus 25 provides the solution. For the Israelites, a week could be a week of years: After seven Sabbaths/weeks of years (forty-nine years), jubilee freedom came (Leviticus 25:8–10). Similarly, the "seventy weeks" of Daniel 9 are a large-scale jubilee period. Freedom could come after seventy weeks of years, which totals 490 years. The reference in Daniel 9:25 to seven weeks (forty-nine years) at the beginning of the seventy weeks, reinforces this interpretation that the seventy weeks represent a period leading up to a kind of jubilee.

Step 6: Find the end of the 490 years

If you begin the 490 years at 457 B.C., then this period ends in A.D. 34. To figure this, you must take into account the fact that there was no year 0 between B.C. and A.D. time. In other words, when the year 1 B.C. expired, the next year was A.D. 1, not the year 0. So subtract 457 from 490, which yields 33, but then add 1 to compensate for the missing year 0, and you arrive at A.D. 34. Daniel 9:25, 26 says that the Messiah would come at the beginning of the last week of years—in other words, seven years before A.D. 34, which is A.D. 27.

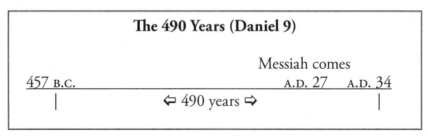

The 490 Years (Daniel 9)

Messiah comes

457 B.C.   A.D. 27   A.D. 34

⇐ 490 years ⇒

Step 7: Recognize that the end of Daniel 9 refers to events that would happen after the 490 years, but still during the 2,300 days

Gabriel told Daniel that "an anointed one" (the Messiah-the Christ) was to be "cut off" and have "nothing," and then Jerusalem would be destroyed along with its temple (Daniel 9:26, NRSV). Daniel 9:27 says the Messiah would confirm a covenant with many (compare Matthew 26:28) and then make the earthly sacrificial system cease—that is, bring an end to its significance (see Matthew 27:51; Hebrews 7–10) at the end of the 490 years. Then, " 'on the wing of abominations will come one who makes desolate, even until a complete destruction, one that is decreed, is poured out on the one who makes desolate' " (Daniel 9:27).

In Daniel 9, the immediate context of the desolating/appalling abomination is the destruction of the second temple (Herod's temple) in Jerusalem by the imperial Roman army under Titus in A.D. 70, a few decades after Jesus' crucifixion (A.D. 31). Jesus spoke of this event when He warned, " 'When you see the abomination of desolation which was spoken of through Daniel the prophet, standing in the holy place (let the reader understand), then let those who are in Judea flee to the mountains' " (Matthew 24:15, 16). Because the early Christians recognized the fulfillment of this sign when the pagan banners of the Roman army stood in the holy space that extended outside the walls of Jerusalem from the temple area, they escaped the destruction of the city.

This language of Daniel 9:27 also ties in to the rest of the story that we already know from Daniel 8:11–13, especially in the words of verse 13—" 'transgression that makes desolate' " (NRSV)—during the latter part of the 2,300 days. Here Daniel 8 refers to some kind of earthly false worship that the vertical phase of the Roman little horn—the Church of Rome—would put in place of the earthly sacrificial and priestly system that Christ had made to cease. Now we can better understand why Daniel 8 would portray imperial and papal Rome together under the same little-horn symbol: Both would perpetrate desolating transgression/abomination after Christ's first coming. While Daniel 9:27 has imperial Rome in the foreground, the Church of Rome is in the background (compare Matthew 24:15–29, which speaks of a time of great tribulation).

Step 8: Recognize that the 2,300 days, like the 490 days, must represent years

Now we know several things:

- The sanctuary that is "justified" at the end of the 2,300 days must be God's heavenly sanctuary, where Christ is now ministering (Hebrews 7–10). We reach this conclusion because God "justifies" the sanctuary to remedy the abominations committed by the vertical (papal) phase of the little horn, which occur after the earthly temple was destroyed in A.D. 70.

- The 2,300 days of Daniel 8 and the 490 years of Daniel 9 both began in the time of the Medo-Persian Empire.

- The 2,300 days reach beyond the 490 years, through a time when the Church of Rome would set up false worship, to a time when God would solve this problem. So the 2,300-day period reaches from Medo-Persian times all the way through the era of domination by the Church of Rome. Therefore, the 2,300 "evenings-mornings" (days) must be longer than the 490 years and must represent years, as days stand for years elsewhere in some symbolic time prophecies (Numbers 14:34; Ezekiel 4:6).

Step 9: See how the 490 years overlap the first part of the 2,300 years

Since in explaining "the vision," Gabriel gave a beginning point only for the 490 years (Daniel 9:23, 25), the 2,300 years must begin at the same point. The language of Daniel 9:24 agrees with the idea that the 490 years are the first part of the 2,300 years: " 'Seventy weeks have been decreed for your people.' " The Hebrew word translated "decreed" here is not used elsewhere in the Bible. However, it is fairly common in rabbinic Hebrew, where it most often has the basic meaning "cut (off)." The objects that were cut could be things such as animal parts, but the word could also be used to speak of cutting a verse into two verses.[3]

"Determined" or "decreed" is an extended meaning; in ancient times a legal decision or decree by a government was regarded as something that was "cut" (compare our idiom "cut a deal"). The Hebrew word is just right for Daniel 9:24 because both the basic and extended meanings apply: The "seventy weeks" were "cut off" for the Jewish people from the beginning of the 2,300 years and they were "determined/decreed" for the Jewish people.

When Does the Pre-Advent Judgment Begin? (Daniel 8; 9)

From 457 B.C., when the Jews began to restore the city of God's ancient earthly temple, the 490 years reached forward to the establishment of Christ's first phase of atonement in the heavenly temple: mediation. The 2,300 years reach forward to the beginning of His second phase of atonement: judgment.

Step 10: Find the end of the 2,300 years

Now that we have a beginning date, 457 B.C., we can easily figure out when the heavenly sanctuary is to be cleansed according to Daniel 8:14. Going forward 2,300 years from 457 B.C. without a zero year, we come to A.D. 1844, soon after the civil power of the Church of Rome ended. It makes sense that a heavenly judgment meant to solve problems created by the Roman power would begin when the period of this power's domination, which created the problems, had ended—in other words, in 1844, after the 1798 end of Rome's domination, when Napoleon's general Berthier took the pope captive.

The implications of our conclusion for modern Christians are staggering. We are living at the time of the pre-Advent, Day of Atonement judgment, just before Jesus comes again to conquer planet Earth and set up His eternal kingdom! The messages of the three angels in Revelation 14 directly apply to us. While Christ, our heavenly High Priest, is justifying/vindicating the sanctuary, representing God's holy character, we should be participating in this event by demonstrating our loyalty through keeping the commandments of God and the faith of Jesus.

---

1. Adapted from Roy Gane, *Altar Call* (Berrien Springs, Mich.: Diadem, 1999), 280–97; compare Clifford Goldstein, *1844 Made Simple* (Nampa, Idaho: Pacific Press®, 1988).

2. Siegfried H. Horn and Lynn H. Wood, *The Chronology of Ezra 7* (Hagerstown, Md.: Review and Herald, 1953, 1970), especially 115, 127; compare *The Seventh-day Adventist Bible Commentary*, Francis D. Nichol, ed. (Hagerstown, Md.: Review and Herald, 1955), 3:100–108; Brempong Owusu-Antwi, *The Chronology of Daniel 9:24-27*, Adventist Theological Society Dissertation Series 2 (Berrien Springs, Mich.: Adventist Theological Society, 1995), 295–299.

3. Marcus Jastrow, *A Dictionary of the Targumim, the Talmud Babli and Yerushalmi, and the Midrashic Literature* (New York: Judaica Press, 1975), 513.

CHAPTER 9

Answers to Objections Regarding Judgment Beginning in 1844

Naturally, not everyone agrees that God is carrying out a pre-Advent judgment that began in 1844. Below are some of the most important objections raised by those who do not accept the line of evidence and logic presented in the previous chapter. What difference does it make? If the judgment began in 1844, it is going on in heaven now, which means that we have the privilege and responsibility of participating during the time of the last great phase of atonement just before Jesus comes again. If this is not the case, we are not living in this special time, the messages of the three angels in Revelation 14 do not especially apply to us, and human beings may continue to live on planet Earth in sin and misery for another thousand years or more. If so, maybe we should start preparing for Y3K!

Objection 1: The day-represents-a-year principle is invalid.

If the 2,300 "days" in Daniel 8:14 represent something other than years, the prophecy doesn't span 2,300 years nor does it point to 1844. What are the alternatives? If the period prophesied is 2,300 literal, twenty-four-hour days, it means that just 6.3 years lead up to the justifying of the sanctuary. What then would be the starting point, and when would the 6.3 years end? If we take seriously the text of Daniel 8, according to which the 2,300 "days" covers the span of the vision from the Medo-Persian period through Hellenistic domination into the Roman era and on to the "time of the end" (verse 17), the result is absurdity. Obviously, the reigns of some individual monarchs alone, not to mention the Medo-Persian period itself, covered many more than 6.3 years.

Furthermore, why would Daniel be as upset as Daniel 9 portrays him about a delay in the restoration of the sanctuary of a mere 6.3 years? That would be like us complaining when someone promises us peace in the Middle East in less than a decade. (Don't hold your breath!)

Are there any other alternatives? In the next chapter, we will refute the interpretation that the 2,300 "days" are really half days and are prophetic of the period when Antiochus IV Epiphanes persecuted the Jews in Jerusalem during the second century B.C. Could the "days" represent literal weeks or months? There is simply no evidence in the Bible for those suggestions.

There is, however, solid evidence for "days" representing literal years in the symbolic time prophecies of Daniel—a principle of interpretation that is crucial for the historical/historicist (as opposed to the preterist or futurist) approach to Daniel.[1]

1. To begin with, the Hebrew word *yom*, "day," can be used for a period of time other than a day of twenty-four hours. Scholars have recognized verses in which the plural of *yom* means "year."[2] Here are some examples:

- "The man Elkanah went up with all his household to offer to the LORD the *yearly sacrifice*"— literally, "*sacrifice of the days*" (1 Samuel 1:21, emphasis supplied; compare 2:19; 20:6).
- " 'Dwell with me and be a father and a priest to me, and I will give you ten pieces of silver *a year*' "—literally, "*for the days*" (Judges 17:10, emphasis supplied).
- "And the number of days that David lived in the country of the Philistines was *a year* and four months"—literally, "*days* and four months" (1 Samuel 27:7, emphasis supplied).

2. In Numbers 14:34, God specified punishment for the rebellion of the Israelites, who refused to take the Promised Land because they believed the ten faithless scouts (see Numbers 13). The punishment fit the crime: " ' "According to the number of days which you spied out the land, forty days, for every day you shall bear your guilt

a year, even forty years, and you shall know My opposition." ' " The Israelites were to wander for forty years in the wilderness, one year for each day of the scouts' mission.

3. In Ezekiel 4, the Lord commanded the prophet Ezekiel to perform symbolic actions to impress on his people the gravity of their situation. Significantly for our study, Ezekiel was a contemporary of Daniel. God told him to lie on one side for the number of days that corresponded to the years of iniquity committed by the northern kingdom of Israel, and then to do the same on the other side for the years of Judah's iniquity: " 'As for you, lie down on your left side, and lay the iniquity of the house of Israel on it; you shall bear their iniquity for the number of days that you lie on it. For I have assigned you a number of days corresponding to the years of their iniquity, three hundred and ninety days; thus you shall bear the iniquity of the house of Israel. When you have completed these, you shall lie down a second time, but on your right side, and bear the iniquity of the house of Judah; I have assigned it to you for forty days, a day for each year' " (Ezekiel 4:4–6).

4. In chapter 7 of this book we noted that the "seventy weeks" of Daniel 9:24–27 are seventy sabbatical-year cycles of seven years each, comprising a total of 490 years, which comprise ten jubilee cycles of forty-nine years each (see Leviticus 25).[3] In this case we can verify historically the result of applying the day/year principle: Jesus began His ministry in A.D. 27 at the beginning of the last "week" of years of the 490 years that stretch from 457 B.C. to A.D. 34. So Christ came exactly when Daniel said He would, *if* we understand Daniel's "weeks" to be weeks of years rather than of days. The seventy weeks of Daniel 9:24–27 are the first segment of the 2,300 evenings-mornings of Daniel 8:14. If the former represent years, then the latter must also.

Notice that the precision of Daniel's prediction of Christ in 9:24–27 is a major blow to those who do not accept accurate predictive prophecy from God. This prophecy reaches far beyond the second century B.C., when many scholars believe that the book of Daniel was written, and even beyond the date of some manuscripts of Daniel belonging to the Dead Sea Scrolls. So, the prophecy pinpointing the timing of the Messiah's coming could not possibly have been history written after the fact as if it were a prediction.

5. In keeping with the symbolic nature of the prophecies of Daniel 7 and 8, we would expect the time periods in these chapters to be sym-

bolic also. Indeed, just as the symbolic animals in these chapters are unusual, so also the prophecies present the time periods in unusual terminology, apparently to emphasize their symbolic nature. Thus Daniel 8:14 specifies 2,300 "evenings-mornings," an abnormal expression for 2,300 days (on which we will see more in our next chapter).

Daniel 7:25 speaks of "a time, times, and half a time" during which the little-horn power would persecute the people of God. The Aramaic word 'iddan, translated "time," is not a usual word for a particular unit of time, such as a day, week, month, or year. But its meaning becomes clear when we look at Daniel 4, where the prophet uses the same word for the "seven times" (or "seven periods of time") that would pass over Nebuchadnezzar before his mind would be restored (verses 16, 32). Verse 34 says, " 'At the end of *that period* [literally "the days," that is, "the years"; see above] I, Nebuchadnezzar, raised my eyes toward heaven, and my reason returned to me' " (emphasis supplied). So if "times" means years here, the same meaning would work in Daniel 7:25—three and one-half years.

Comparison with Revelation 12 confirms this interpretation of Daniel's "times." In speaking of the same period of persecution, this chapter uses Daniel's terminology of three-and-a-half "times" (verse 14), but it also directly specifies what that amounts to: 1,260 days (verse 6). So, three-and-a-half times equals three-and-a-half years at 360 days per year. See also Revelation 11:2, 3; 13:5, where this period is given as "forty-two months." At thirty days per month, forty-two months equals 1,260 days.

Now we can better understand the connection in Daniel 12 between "a time, times, and half a time" (verse 7), which we now know is 1,260 days, and two longer periods that are explicitly numbered in "days" rather than "times": "1,290 days" (verse 11) and "1,335 days" (verse 12). The contexts in both Daniel and Revelation describe extensive persecution by a major religious power. Clearly, then, the 1,260 days cannot be 1,260 literal, twenty-four-hour periods but must be prophetic/symbolic "days"—in other words, 1,260 literal years. Indeed, we have identified the persecutor as the Church of Rome, and the persecutions carried out by that church extended over many centuries.

To dismiss the time periods in Daniel as merely symbolic and therefore not to be connected to real spans of specific historical time would not do justice to this kind of prophetic literature. First, the symbolic image, animals, and horns of Daniel 2, 7, and 8 represent actual historical powers, some of which the prophet explicitly identifies as such in his book (2:38; 8:20, 21). Second, we have found that in Numbers 14:34 and Ezekiel 4:6, specific numbers of "days" are used symbolically for the same number of real years. Third, we have seen that in Daniel 9:24–27, the time frame of the seventy weeks matches the historical chronology of Christ's first coming.

In the context of Daniel 9:24–27, the "weeks" are so obviously sabbatical year periods, that is, weeks of years, that the day-year principle hardly seems to be in effect. However, elsewhere in the Hebrew Bible the word for "week" denotes a week of days. The terminology for the sabbatical years in Leviticus 25:8 is related to that of Daniel but different—literally "sabbaths of years": " ' "You are also to count off seven sabbaths of years for yourself, seven times seven years, so that you have the time [literally "days"] of the seven sabbaths of years, namely, forty-nine years." ' " So again we see that unusual use of terminology in Daniel, in this case "weeks" for weeks of years, is symbolic and alerts us to the presence of the day-year principle.

Objection 2: Daniel 9:25 does not refer to the decree of Artaxerxes I in 457 B.C.

If " ' "the issuing of a decree to restore and rebuild Jerusalem" ' " (Daniel 9:25) does not refer to the decree issued by the Medo-Persian king Artaxerxes I in the seventh year of his reign (Ezra 7), which was 457 B.C., there must be another beginning point for the seventy-week prophecy. If so, there is obviously another ending point and the prophecy wouldn't accurately pinpoint the time of Christ's first coming. This would cast serious doubt on the day-year principle and would undermine the basis for our calculation of the 2,300 evenings-mornings period (Daniel 8:14), which begins with this decree.

One objection to identifying the Daniel 9 decree as that of Artaxerxes is that according to a number of translations and commentaries, it was Cyrus who decreed that Jerusalem should be rebuilt (c. 536 B.C.) according to Isaiah 44:28. Therefore, the 2,300 years didn't end in 1844.

However, the New Revised Standard Version has the correct translation of Isaiah 44:28, according to which it was God, not

Cyrus, who said of Jerusalem, " 'It shall be rebuilt.' " This translation preserves the pattern of Hebrew syntax that runs through verses 24–28. The rebuilding of Jerusalem began with Cyrus (Ezra 1:1–4; see also 6:3–5), continued with Darius I (6:6–12), who consciously followed the precedent Cyrus had set, and culminated under the decree of Artaxerxes I, as indicated by Ezra 6:14: "And they finished building according to the command of the God of Israel and the decree of Cyrus, Darius, and Artaxerxes king of Persia."

Cyrus did play an important role in the restoration process ordained by God as prophesied in Isaiah 45:13: " 'He [Cyrus] will build My city, and will let My exiles go free.' " But it was the decree of Artaxerxes (Ezra 7:11–26), unlike the earlier decrees of Cyrus and Darius, that explicitly included concern for the city of Jerusalem itself, not just the temple in Jerusalem. Artaxerxes' decree mandated Jerusalem's restoration as the civil judicial and administrative center and therefore, by implication, as the capital of the Jewish people (Ezra 7).[4] "From the point of view of both the Jews and the royal power, the principal mission entrusted to Ezra was in the legal realm. He was in fact ordered to appoint judges and magistrates 'to administer justice for the whole people of Transeuphrates'; exemplary punishment was promised to any who did not carry out 'the Law of your God—which is the law of the king' (7:25)."[5]

Notice that Daniel 9:25 speaks of restoring and rebuilding Jerusalem; the city is the direct object of both verbs. So although "restore" here literally means "cause to return," it is not speaking of Cyrus causing the Jews to return to their homeland. Rather, it has to do with causing the city of Jerusalem to return to its former state.

Here is a second objection to the decree of Artaxerxes I. According to Daniel 9:25, the seventy weeks begin when a decree goes forth " 'to restore and rebuild Jerusalem.' " The decree of Artaxerxes I in 457 B.C. didn't explicitly call for rebuilding the walls of Jerusalem. In fact, that happened later, under Nehemiah, who received authorization from Artaxerxes in the king's twentieth year, 444 B.C. (Nehemiah 2). Therefore, some would say, it is faulty to use 457 B.C. as the starting point of the seventy-week and 2,300-year prophecies.

However, careful comparison with similar terminology elsewhere in the Bible shows that the decree of Artaxerxes fits the prophetic specification even better than we thought! The Hebrew of Daniel 9:25 has the Hiphil (causative) of *shub*, "to bring back, restore," combined with *banah*, "build." These two verbs are also used together with a city as their direct object in 2 Kings 14:22: "He built Elath and restored it to Judah, after the king slept with his fathers" (compare 2 Chronicles 26:2). Here restoration of a city means *restoration of its ownership to a political entity.* This idea also appears in 1 Kings 20:34, "And Ben-hadad said to him, 'The cities which my father took from your father I will restore, and you shall make streets for yourself in Damascus, as my father made in Samaria.' "

This last verse is a particularly interesting parallel to Daniel 9:25 because restoration of ownership by a king precedes a public works project by the party to whom the city is restored (compare Daniel 9:25—" 'it will be built again, with plaza and moat' "). It was the decree of Artaxerxes I, recorded in Ezra 7, that handed Jerusalem back to the Jews in the sense of giving them autonomous civil control of the city (under the Persian Empire, of course). This apparently implied permission to restore the city's public works infrastructure, including its walls, which Ezra and those who returned with him began to do until they ran into opposition (Ezra 4:11–16), and which Nehemiah, with permission from Artaxerxes, completed.[6]

A third objection to the decree of Artaxerxes I is that Ezra 7 speaks of the seventh year of a different Artaxerxes. There were four Medo-Persian kings named Artaxerxes:[7] Artaxerxes I, 465–424/423; Artaxerxes II, 405–359; Artaxerxes III, 359–338; and Artaxerxes IV, 338–336. However, Nehemiah 13:6 rules out the last two as the monarch who ruled during the time of Ezra and Nehemiah by referring to the thirty-second year of Artaxerxes. Artaxerxes III and IV didn't reign that long. Of Artaxerxes I and II, the historical context of the former fits the period of Ezra-Nehemiah the best.

Amelie Kuhrt describes the vigorous actions of Artaxerxes I to meet a threat from the Athenians, who supported an Egyptian revolt against the Persians: "Artaxerxes moved fast to counteract them: an Achaemenid general, Megabazos, was sent to crush the Egyptian revolt, which he did brutally, annihilating the Egyptian rebels and the Athenian contingent (Thucydides 1.110). Archaeological evidence from several sites in the Levant suggests that new fortified garrison-points were set up to strengthen Persia's defenses. The missions of the

Achaemenid Jewish courtiers, Ezra and Nehemiah, to Jerusalem (perhaps to be dated to 458 and 445 respectively) may well be linked to this vigorous Persian effort to beat back the Greek threat."[8]

Kuhrt's mention of 458 B.C. as the possible date for the mission of Ezra is in harmony with her chronology, according to which this would be the seventh year of Artaxerxes I (Ezra 7:7). Other eminent historians also give 458 B.C. as the date of the decree of Artaxerxes and the mission of Ezra.[9] This is one year earlier than the 457 B.C. date that we have used—a slight difference, especially considering that the ancient years overlapped our years, so that one year in the ancient calendar would have overlapped our calendar's 458 and 457 B.C. Siegfried Horn and Lyn Wood examined closely the correlations between ancient documents dated to the reign of Artaxerxes that used different calendar systems. They concluded that according to the Jewish calendar that Ezra would have used, the decree of Artaxerxes and Ezra's trip actually occurred in 457 B.C.[10] William Shea explains that according to the Persian spring-to-spring calendar,

> Artaxerxes' seventh year began in the spring of 458 B.C. and ended in the spring of 457 B.C. Thus by the Persian calendar, Ezra would have begun his journey from Babylon in the spring of 458 B.C. and arrived in Jerusalem in the summer of that same year.
>
> The Jews, however, considered the new year to begin in the fall, according to the civil calendar by which they kept track of the reigns of their kings and those of other nations. . . . Thus by the Jewish civil calendar, Artaxerxes' seventh year would have begun in the fall of 458 B.C. and ended in the fall of 457 B.C. By this reckoning, Ezra would have begun his journey to Jerusalem in the spring of 457 B.C., arriving there in the summer of the same year.[11]

Objection 3: We have no historical source that dates the death of Christ to A.D. 31.

Daniel 9:27 says that the Messiah would put an end to (the significance of) the earthly sacrificial system for (the second) half of the final week of years—that is, about A.D. 31 if these 490 years reach from 457 B.C. to A.D. 34. Nowhere does the New Testament or any other source give a specific year for Jesus' crucifixion. We know from the Gospels that He died on a Friday of Passover during the early years of Pontius Pilate's term as the Roman procurator—that is, sometime between A.D. 29 and 33. Of course, A.D. 31 falls within this range. Although it has been shown that a Passover Friday crucifixion in A.D. 30 or 31 is possible in light of astronomical calculations, even astronomy has not proven conclusive in nailing down the date of this event.[12] How then can we be sure that Christ accurately fulfilled the seventy-weeks prophecy of Daniel 9:24–27? Doubt about His fulfillment of this prophecy would also cast doubt on our interpretation of the 2,300 evenings-mornings of Daniel 8:14.

We don't need confirmation of Christ's death in A.D. 30 or 31 because we have confirmation of His baptism in A.D. 27, at the beginning of the last of Daniel's seventy weeks of years (seven plus sixty-two "weeks"—in other words, 483 years after 457 B.C.; see Daniel 9:25, 26). Jesus was baptized and began His public ministry "in the fifteenth year of the reign of Tiberius Caesar" (Luke 3:1). It is well known from secular historical sources that Tiberius became sole emperor of Rome (after having been co-ruler in the Roman provinces) when Augustus died on August 19, A.D. 14. Luke probably followed the usual Jewish method of dating at that time, which reckoned the first year of a king's reign as the portion of the year that came before the first New Year's Day (in autumn, about mid-October) of his reign. So the time between August 19 and October of A.D. 14 would have been counted as Tiberius's first year. The emperor's second year would have been the Jewish civil year covering October of A.D. 14 to October of A.D. 15. Continuing in this way, Tiberius's fifteenth year would have reached from the autumn of A.D. 27 to the autumn of A.D. 28. The end of Daniel's 483 years was A.D. 27, falling within the range of Tiberius's fifteenth year. Jesus kept His appointment with Daniel's prophecy![13]

To conclude this chapter, we have found the day-year principle and 457 B.C. as the starting point of the 490- and 2,300-year prophecies of Daniel 8 and 9 to be solid. In addition, Daniel's seventy-week prophecy reaches to the time of Christ, which means that it extends far beyond any possible date when the book of Daniel could have been written. So we must conclude that Daniel 9 definitely contains real, accurate, predictive prophecy. This supports the idea that Daniel's other prophecies (Daniel 2; 7; 8; and 11; 12) accurately cover a sweep of history that begins in the past and reaches through our time into the future, to the end of the present era and the commencement of the new age of Christ's eternal kingdom.

---

1. See the defense of the day-year principle by Desmond Ford in *Daniel* (Nashville: Southern Publishing Association, 1978), 300–305 (Appendix F) and William Shea's major study in *Selected Studies on Prophetic Interpretation,* Daniel and Revelation Committee Series 1, Frank H. Holbrook, ed. (Silver Spring, Md.: Biblical Research Institute, 1992), 67–110. See also Gerhard Pfandl, *Daniel: The Seer of Babylon* (Hagerstown, Md.: Review and Herald, 2004), 60–62.

2. Ludwig Koehler and Walter Baumgartner, *The Hebrew and Aramaic Lexicon of the Old Testament* (Leiden: Brill, 2001), 1:400, 401.

3. See Ben Zion Wacholder, "Chronomessianism: The Timing of Messianic Movements and the Calendar of Sabbatical Cycles, *Hebrew Union College Annual* 46 (1975): 202–209.

4. Roy Gane, *Altar Call* (Berrien Springs, Mich.: Diadem, 1999), 289, 290.

5. Pierre Briant, *From Cyrus to Alexander: A History of the Persian Empire* (Winona Lake, Ind.: Eisenbrauns, 2002), 584.

6. Arthur Ferch, "Commencement Date for the Seventy Week Prophecy," in *The Seventy Weeks, Leviticus, and the Nature of Prophecy,* Daniel and Revelation Committee Series 3, Frank H. Holbrook, ed. (Silver Spring, Md.: Biblical Research Institute, 1986), 64–74; Brempong Owusu-Antwi, *The Chronology of Daniel 9:24-27,* Adventist Theological Society Dissertation Series 2 (Berrien Springs, Mich.: Adventist Theological Society, 1995), 133–138, 290–295, 299–303.

7. Amelie Kuhrt, *The Ancient Near East c. 3000–330 BC* (London and New York: Routledge, 1995), 2:648.

8. Ibid., 671, 672.

9. *A History of the Jewish People,* H. H. Ben-Sasson, ed. (Cambridge, Mass.: Harvard University Press, 1976), 173; *The Cambridge History of Judaism,* W. D. Davies and Louis Finkelstein, eds. (Cambridge: Cambridge University Press, 1984), 73; Briant, 583. Note that we have precise dating based on ancient records of astronomical phenomena (especially eclipses) that correlate with regnal years from Neo-Babylonian times onward. Consequently, scholars can date many events in the reigns of monarchs from this era to the *day* when they occurred.

10. Siegfried H. Horn and Lynn H. Wood, *The Chronology of Ezra 7* (Hagerstown, Md.: Review and Herald, 1953, 1970), especially 115, 127; see also *The Seventh-day Adventist Bible Commentary,* Francis D. Nichol, ed. (Hagerstown, Md.: Review and Herald, 1955), 3:100–109; Owusu-Antwi, 295–299.

11. William H. Shea, *Daniel 7–12: Prophecies of the End Time,* The Abundant Life Bible Amplifier (Nampa, Idaho: Pacific Press®, 1996), 65.

12. C. Mervyn Maxwell, *God Cares: The Message of Daniel for You and Your Family* (Nampa, Idaho: Pacific Press®, 1981) 1:257–263; Owusu-Antwi, 310–323.

13. *The Seventh-day Adventist Bible Commentary,* 5:243–247, explains this chronology in detail.

CHAPTER

More Answers to Objections: Rome Versus Antiochus

In the previous chapter, I responded to objections to the interpretation of the "2,300 evenings-mornings" prophecy of Daniel 8:14 as 2,300 years running from 457 B.C. to A.D. 1844. In the present chapter, we'll consider another kind of objection, one that challenges the dating of the prophecies in Daniel and calls their basic credibility into serious question. Similarly, in court, if you can't answer a person's arguments, you can win the case if you show that the individual can't be trusted—or that the person is not even who he says he is.

A widespread scholarly theory holds that Daniel's prophecies regarding the little-horn power and its equivalent in Daniel 7–12 were actually written in response to the crisis the Seleucid king Antiochus IV Epiphanes (reigned 175 B.C. to 164/3 B.C.) caused the Jews. This theory says that someone other than Daniel wrote the book that bears his name and that it was written after the events "prophesied" in it had already occurred. If this approach is on target, the 2,300 evenings-mornings were fulfilled in the distant past, so there is no pre-Advent judgment going on right now.

The majority of scholars today accept and teach the theory just described, as anyone can easily see by looking at commentaries on Daniel. In most of these commentaries, Antiochus is pervasive and shapes the entire framework of prophetic interpretation. A number of scholars have lost sight of the fact that the theory is a theory; they treat it as an assumed fact or a fixed dogma that is beyond critique.[1]

Origins of interpretations

Where did the interpretation that identifies the little horn as Antiochus Epiphanes originate?

The now-frequent application of the fourth kingdom of Dan. 2 and 7 to the Hellenistic period, and thus of the little horn of Dan. 7 to Antiochus Epiphanes, has generally been traced back to Porphyry (A.D. 233–c. 304), a Neoplatonist and a defender of paganism. Alarmed at the onward spread of Christianity, and sensing the key position occupied by prophecy in early Christian thinking, Porphyry attempted to parry the force of Daniel's prophecy by contending that the book was not a prophecy written by Daniel in the 6th century B.C., but a deceptive historical sketch, penned by a later writer in the time of the Maccabees. In other words, Porphyry charged that the book was fabricated after the historical events had taken place, but was couched in the future tense as if a prediction.[2]

The present book supports the historicist approach to understanding the prophecies of Daniel. Non-Christians find this approach threatening because it identifies Jesus as the Messiah by the timing of His first coming (see Daniel 9:24–27). The Church of Rome finds it threatening because it profiles this power as God's little-horn enemy. Many Protestant Christians continue bowing to Roman traditional authority by worshiping on the Roman Sunday and wish to legitimize the Church of Rome and unite with it even more, so they also dislike the historical approach.

In addition, for most Christians—Catholics and Protestants, including evangelicals—following the historical accuracy of Daniel's prophecies through to their logical conclusion that a pre-Advent judgment began in A.D. 1844 is unacceptable. They don't like this interpretation, which only Seventh-day Adventists hold, because it is associated with William Miller's now discredited prediction that

Christ's second advent would take place in 1844. Many Christians think the Seventh-day Adventist Church, which came out of the nineteenth-century Millerite movement, made up the pre-Advent judgment idea to save face by retaining the date 1844 but changing the event to a heavenly one, which is beyond the ability of human beings to disprove.[3]

But of course, one can't disprove an interpretation of the Bible by pointing either to its origin or to its connection to a discredited idea. If such were the case, consistency would suggest that Christian scholars should dismiss the theory that Antiochus was the little horn solely because it originated with Porphyry, who was a pagan, anti-Christian polemicist. We should judge interpretations of the Bible by their consistency with the principles of interpretation that arise from the Bible itself.

The book of Daniel's long-range prophecies of a succession of world empires that reaches far beyond the time of Daniel, even far beyond the time of Antiochus IV Epiphanes (see chapters 2; 7; 8), and that book's predictions regarding the Messiah (chapter 9:24–27) have been proven accurate. And the Seventh-day Adventist view of the 2,300 evenings-mornings prophecy is consistent with the interpretation of these other prophecies. Shouldn't these facts be sufficient reason to believe in a heavenly, pre-Advent judgment event?

Why Antiochus IV Epiphanes isn't the little horn

Here are some serious problems that rule out identification of Antiochus IV Epiphanes with the little horn:[4]

1. In Daniel 7, the little horn arises from the fourth empire, which is Rome.[5] The second century B.C. Seleucid king Antiochus IV Epiphanes was a ruler of one of the four divisions of the Greek Empire, which came before Rome. So Antiochus cannot be the "little horn." He appeared on the scene centuries too early.

One Sabbath evening when my brother and I were young, our parents played "twenty questions" (a Bible guessing game) with us. My brother stumped the rest of us with a Bible character that none of us could guess, so we gave up. He then informed us that the character was Abraham Lincoln! My brother knew that there was an Abraham in the Bible, that in Bible times men wore beards, and that Abraham Lincoln looked ancient and wore a beard. But although

Lincoln loved the Bible and used biblical language in his speeches, the Bible doesn't mention him. Putting him there was an anachronism. Identifying the second-century B.C. Antiochus as the little horn of Daniel's prophecy when Daniel said the horn would arise from the Roman Empire is also an anachronism.

To overcome the difficulty that the little horn grows out of the fourth empire, preterist scholars split up Media and Persia, saying that the four empires are Babylon, Media, Persia, and Greece. This makes Greece the fourth empire and so Antiochus can be the little horn, which came from the fourth empire.

Nice try, but not so fast. Media and Persia had already combined into a single empire by the time they conquered Babylon, and the book of Daniel speaks of one kingdom of the Medes and Persians, which shared one system of law (see Daniel 5:28; 6:8, 12, 15; 8:20; compare Esther 1:3, 14, 18, 19; 10:2). Furthermore, the Babylonian "Dynastic Prophecy" lists the empires that ruled Babylonia before Macedonia/Greece did as Assyria, Babylon, and Elam (Persia). This Babylonian text contains no separate Media.[6] Don't you think the Babylonians would remember who had ruled them?

There is a basic difference between the way preterist and historicist scholars read the book of Daniel to identify the little horn. Many preterists begin with Daniel 11, explaining a large chunk of this chapter by identifying the evil "king of the North" (the "despicable person" of verses 21 and following) with Antiochus. They say that Antiochus is the big bad guy here who does away with regular worship (which they say is the regular sacrifice in Jerusalem) and sets up the abomination of desolation (11:31). Then they read that identification back into Daniel 7 and 8, where it is the little horn that does these things. The logical result is to assert that Antiochus fulfills the little-horn symbol. However, doing so twists Daniel 7 and 8 out of shape. Granted that Daniel 11 is supposed to help explain the earlier prophecies, but an explanation should agree with what it explains!

The historicist approach of the present book, on the other hand, reads Daniel forward, allowing the earlier chapters (2; 7; 8) to unfold the sequence of powers naturally, forming a clear framework within which to interpret Daniel 11. "Since Daniel 2 is the more simple prophecy and Daniel 7 adds detail and is the more complex, it seems natural and logical to begin with the more simple prophecy and work on through the book to the more complex, adding the details presented by each successive prophecy."[7]

The result doesn't either ignore or bend Daniel 11. Rather, it places this chapter into the perspective established by the book of Daniel itself.[8]

2. Another problem is that Antiochus was only one king in the middle of a line of Seleucid rulers. And while he did persecute the Jews for a time, his forays into Egypt, Palestine, and elsewhere soon ended in failure. Although he enjoyed some initial success in Egypt, he left that country and withdrew his army simply because the Roman ambassador, C. Popilius Laenas, told him that the Roman Senate wanted him to get out.[9] He was afraid of Rome because this emerging power had decisively defeated his father, Antiochus III, who was much greater than he was. And rather than conquering Palestine, Antiochus IV lost it to the Jews under the leadership of the Maccabees. He died while fighting in the East. The bottom line is that Antiochus was a certified, card-carrying loser. He hardly fits the profile of the great little horn in Daniel 7 and 8 that arises "in the latter period" of the rule of the Hellenistic kingdoms (8:23) and surpasses all of them.

3. From His perspective in the first century A.D. (see Matthew 24:15, 16), Jesus interpreted the "abomination of desolation," or "desolating/appalling sacrilege"—a blasphemous religious object or practice that Daniel said the little-horn power would set up (Daniel 8:12, 13; 9:27; 11:31; 12:11)—as still future. The book of Revelation also looks to the future when speaking of the period of domination by an evil power that is symbolized in Daniel by the little horn.

Daniel 7:25	Revelation 12:6	Revelation 12:14	Revelation 13:5
3 and 1/2 times	1,260 days (3 and 1/2 years)	3 and 1/2 times	42 months (3 and 1/2 years)

In Revelation, which was written after Jerusalem was destroyed, this period comes *after* the life of Christ on earth: "She gave birth to a son, a male child, who is to rule all the nations with a rod of iron; and her child was caught up to God and to His throne. And the woman fled into the wilderness where she had a place prepared by God, so that there she might be nourished for one thousand two hundred and sixty days" (Revelation 12:5, 6).

It is clear that Christ and the New Testament did not regard the earlier Antiochus as fulfilling the work of the little horn, even though the apocryphal book of 1 Maccabees labels something Antiochus set up on the altar of the Jerusalem temple as the "abomination of desolation" (1:54). Can we accept the interpretation of 1 Maccabees and argue that although in the greater scheme of things Antiochus was a loser, he fulfills the little-horn symbol of Daniel because he loomed large on the horizon of the Jews who were the focus of Daniel's concern? No. Daniel presents the big picture in which the "little horn" is a successor to world-class powers rather than merely a bully to the Jews.

A recent issue of the *Journal of Biblical Literature* contains a fascinating and important article by Steven Weitzman titled "Plotting Antiochus's Persecution." Although Weitzman continues to accept the preterist dogma that Antiochus IV is the little horn of Daniel, he undermines it by strongly supporting the idea that the books of Maccabees are propaganda that fit into a longstanding ancient Near Eastern literary tradition. These books may paint Antiochus's actions in especially dark colors in their attempt to portray the Maccabees as saviors of Jewish religion.[10]

Some say that Antiochus was simply the first of multiple fulfillments of the little horn and that Jesus spoke of one of the other fulfillments. But points 1 and 2 above rule out Antiochus as any kind of fulfillment, even a minor one.[11] He lived at the wrong time, and his career just doesn't fit. Undoubtedly, Antiochus was evil and opposed God, and he certainly did *some* things that Daniel said the little horn would do. But that doesn't make him the little horn.

4. Antiochus persecuted the Jews for 1,080 days. This period doesn't match any of the prophetic time periods given by Daniel. Scholars try to fit this span of time with the 2,300 evenings-mornings of Daniel 8:14 by splitting the 2,300 in half. They say that this verse refers to 2,300 burnt offerings sacrificed "regularly" (compare verses 11–13) morning and evening (compare Numbers 28:4) at the Jerusalem temple in 1,150 literal days, two sacrifices per day.

While many English translations assume that Daniel 8:11–13 speaks of "the regular sacrifice," the original Hebrew text of these verses refers only to "the regularity" (that is, worship that takes place regularly; the so-called "daily"). There is no Hebrew term for "sacrifice" in this context. Even if "the regularity" could be shown to represent the morning and evening burnt offerings at the temple in Jerusalem, these were morning-and-evening, not evening-and-morning as in Daniel 8:14. Additionally, the two sacrifices comprised one unit (see Numbers 28:1–8). Moreover, in Daniel 8:14, "2,300 evenings-mornings" appears to be an abbreviation for "2,300 evenings and 2,300 mornings," as shown by comparison with verse 26—"the evenings and mornings," that is, the 2,300 evenings and the 2,300 mornings, referring to 2,300 full days (compare Deuteronomy 9:25—"the forty days and forty nights").[12]

As we pointed out in chapter 9, "2,300 evenings-mornings"* is an unusual time unit, as are other symbolic units in the time prophecies of Daniel. A similar combination of evening and morning in this order appears in the formulas for the successive day units of the Creation week: "And there was evening and there was morning, one day" (Genesis 1:5; see also verses 8, 13, 19, etc.).[13] Notice that evening followed by morning refers to the cycle of one day, not to two half days. So there is no justification for splitting the 2,300 in half to make 1,150 days, which would come closer to the duration of the persecution perpetrated by Antiochus.

Evening followed by morning also appears in Exodus 27:20, 21: " 'You shall charge the sons of Israel, that they bring you clear oil of beaten olives for the light, to make a lamp burn continually. In the tent of meeting, outside the veil which is before the testimony, Aaron and his sons shall keep it in order from evening to morning before the Lord; it shall be a perpetual statute throughout their generations for the sons of Israel.' "

This passage contains several parallels to Daniel 8: The lamp is burning *continually/regularly* (compare the "regularity"/"continual" in Daniel 8:11–13) in the *sanctuary* (see words for "sanctuary" in Daniel 8:11, 13, 14) from *evening to morning* (compare Daniel 8:14,

---

*Literally "evening-morning," but with large numbers the singular form is used in Hebrew, so the meaning is "evenings-mornings."

26). By providing light throughout the night in the "palace" of the divine King, showing that He is awake, the lamp reminds God's people that "the guardian of Israel neither slumbers nor sleeps!" (Psalm 121:4, The New JPS).[14]

The connection with the sanctuary lamp cycle implies that the 2,300 evenings-mornings could refer to 2,300 nights, that is, the dark portion of 2,300 days (referring to "days" as symbolic twenty-four-hour periods). There is one continuous evening-morning cycle for every twenty-four-hour cycle, so again, there is no support for splitting the 2,300 into half days. The idea of God's keeping watch during the night is prominent in Daniel 6, where God protects the prophet as he spends the night in the lions' den. In Daniel 8, God's people experience a "dark" period of oppression by a succession of powers during 2,300 days/years, but the Lord guards His own during the entire time!

---

1. An extreme example is Louis F. Hartman and Alexander A. Di Lella, *The Book of Daniel*, Anchor Bible 23 (Garden City, New York: Doubleday, 1978).

2. *The Seventh-day Adventist Bible Commentary*, Francis D. Nichol, ed. (Hagerstown, Md.: Review and Herald, 1956) 4:42.

3. See, for example, Tremper Longman III, *Daniel*, NIV Application Commentary (Grand Rapids: Zondervan, 1999), 213.

4. See further William H. Shea, *Selected Studies on Prophetic Interpretation*, Daniel and Revelation Committee Series 1, Frank H. Holbrook, ed. (Silver Spring, Md.: Biblical Research Institute, 1992), 31–66 ("Why Antiochus IV Is Not the Little Horn of Daniel 8"); compare Desmond Ford, *Daniel* (Nashville: Southern Publishing Association, 1978), 164, 188, 191.

5. Hersh Goldwurm expresses the traditional Jewish interpretation of Daniel 7: "The fourth kingdom, represented here by a fearsome unspecified beast, different from all the other beasts, is that of the Roman empire with all of its metamorphoses. This is the view of almost all the commentators and clearly that of our Sages in the *Talmud* and numerous *midrashim.*" *Daniel: A New Translation With a Commentary Anthologized from Talmudic, Midrashic and Rabbinic Sources* (New York: Mesorah, 1979), 199. Accordingly, traditional Jewish identifications of the little horn that comes out of the fourth beast in Daniel 7 have been Titus (Rashi), the institution of the papacy (Abarbanel, Malbim), Islam (Malbim), or a nation that would convert to Islam (Ibn Ezra), all of which come from the Roman period or later (Goldwurm, 202, 203). Identifications of the little horn in Daniel 8 are not the same: the Seleucid kingdom in general (Ibn Ezra), Antiochus IV (Malbim and *Mayenei HaYeshuah*), and the rule of Titus (and Vespasian) over the Roman Empire (Rashi) (Goldwurm, 221, 222).

6. Roy Gane, *Altar Call* (Berrien Springs, Mich.: Diadem, 1999), 299; A. K. Grayson, *Babylonian Historical-Literary Texts* (Toronto: University of Toronto Press, 1975), 24–37.

7. William H. Shea, *Daniel 1–7: Prophecy as History,* The Abundant Life Bible Amplifier (Nampa, Idaho: Pacific Press®, 1996), 132.

8. For this approach to explaining the contours of Daniel 11, see Shea, *Selected Studies,* 53–63; see also William H. Shea, *Daniel 7–12: Prophecies of the End Time,* The Abundant Life Bible Amplifier (Nampa, Idaho: Pacific Press®, 1996), 178–213.

9. See, for example, C. Mervyn Maxwell, *God Cares: The Message of Daniel for You and Your Family* (Nampa, Idaho: Pacific Press®, 1981) 1:159.

10. Steven Weitzman, "Plotting Antiochus's Persecution," *Journal of Biblical Literature* 123 (2004): 219–234.

11. Against Desmond Ford, *Daniel* (Nashville: Southern Publishing Association, 1978), 172, 186, 187.

12. Gane, 284, 285.

13. See Siegfried J. Schwantes, " '*Ereb Boqer* of Daniel 8:14 Re-examined," in *Symposium on Daniel,* Daniel and Revelation Committee Series 2, Frank H. Holbrook, ed. (Silver Spring, Md.: Biblical Research Institute, 1986), 463, 472–474.

14. Roy Gane, *Leviticus, Numbers,* NIV Application Commentary (Grand Rapids: Zondervan, 2004), 557.

CHAPTER 11

Little Horn: Rebel and Antichrist

Daniel 7:9–14 says that the little horn is condemned through the pre-Advent judgment, which involves opening books that presumably record the actions of this power. Why? Such a judgment is not needed to condemn the preceding human empires—Babylon, Media-Persia, Greece, and imperial/pagan Rome. They end simply because they are wicked and there is no question of saving them because they lack any positive connection with the Lord, who alone possesses ultimate power to save. As Jesus said to Nicodemus, " 'He who does not believe has been judged already, because he has not believed in the name of the only begotten Son of God' " (John 3:18). All human beings have sinned, (Romans 3:23), and "the wages of sin is death" (Romans 6:23). So those who have never responded to God's offer of salvation simply die eternal death, just as death-row inmates aren't considered for a stay of execution unless they make an appeal to the governor.

Why wouldn't the little horn be automatically condemned without the convening of a heavenly tribunal that takes the trouble to lay its actions open for inspection? Although the little horn wields coercive force against God's people as other human powers have done (see Daniel 7:25; 8:24; and compare, for example, Daniel 3; 6), the situation differs because the little horn's pretensions transcend secular politics (see Daniel 7:24). It is a religious power. This is shown by the fact that it " ' "will intend to make alterations in times and in law" ' " (Daniel 7:25)—that is, God's covenant laws regarding sacred time and worship.

The little horn comes under the scope of the pre-Advent judgment because it claims a connection with God. Therefore, what it stands for and does affects God's reputation in the world, just as Colonel Oliver North's illegal Iran-contra activities adversely affected the reputation of President Ronald Reagan, under whose administration he was operating. In order to give people an accurate picture of His character, the Lord must show His real relationship to the little horn.

For the same reason, the Lord needed to condemn ancient Israelites and aliens living within the borders of Israel who belonged to His covenant community but who defiled His reputation when they engaged in Molech worship (Leviticus 20:3) or willfully neglected His provision for purifying themselves from corpse contamination (Numbers 19:13, 20). These "transgressions" (rebellious sins) were never forgiven through the Israelite sacrificial systems but they had to be removed from the Israelite sanctuary on the Day of Atonement along with forgivable/forgiven sins (Leviticus 16:16). While removal of the latter sins from the sanctuary benefited the forgiven sinners with moral purification/vindication (verse 30), removal of the transgressions benefited only God. The rebellious sinners had no part in the Day of Atonement judgment in the sense of receiving its benefit, but remained irrevocably condemned.[1]

Rebel

Significantly, the little horn commits "transgression/rebellious sin" (*pesha'*; Daniel 8:12, 13—the same Hebrew term as in Leviticus 16:16). For this it is condemned through the judgment (Daniel 7:11, 22) even though God's sanctuary/reputation is cleansed/vindicated (Daniel 8:14). So the little horn fits the profile of rebellious sinners among God's covenant community who do not receive the benefit of vindication on the Day of Atonement.[2]

In ancient Israel, the most severe defilement of the sanctuary/temple occurred when rebels against the Lord introduced foreign cult objects into the sanctuary itself, as apostate King Manasseh did: "He set the carved image of Asherah that he had made, in the house of which the Lord said to David and to his son Solomon, 'In this house and in

88

Jerusalem, which I have chosen from all the tribes of Israel, I will put My name forever' " (2 Kings 21:7; compare Ezekiel 8). The fact that good King Josiah later had to order the Levites to " 'put the holy ark in the house which Solomon the son of David king of Israel built' " (2 Chronicles 35:3) suggests that Manasseh had removed the ark of the covenant from the Most Holy Place and replaced it with an idolatrous symbol or image of Asherah, a pagan fertility goddess!*

On a larger scale than in the days of Manasseh and Josiah, God's heavenly temple would need to be "justified" (Daniel 8:14) after the little horn put an "appalling rebellion" in place of true worship (verses 11–13) and stopped people from engaging in proper, regular worship of the Lord (Revelation 11:2, 3 says it tramples the court of the temple). "The 'little horn' is particularly guilty because it does not merely disregard part of God's sacrificial system (cf. Num 19:13, 20) and participate in an alternate system (cf. Lev 20:3); it removes part of God's system, i.e. the 'regularity' (so-called 'daily'), and sets up an alternate system (Dan 8:11-13; 11:31; 12:11). Thus the horn would come under the jurisdiction of a court that reviews covenant status."[3]

Again, our identification of the little horn as the Church of Rome (rather than Antiochus IV Epiphanes, who was a pagan ruler) matches perfectly: This church is a professedly Christian power that claims a connection with Christ but denies His heavenly ministry by substituting a confessional, a sacrifice (the Mass), and an earthly priesthood.[4] The Church of Rome developed from the originally faithful early Christian church, so it can claim an unbroken link to the apostles. However, tragically, it fell away from the pure worship authorized by the true God, just as generations of ancient Israelites apostatized and turned to various forms of idolatry, including the mixture of true worship with pagan practice (see the books of Judges, Kings, and Chronicles).

When God's people have turned from Him, especially if they continue to make hypocritical professions of faith, they sully God's reputation. And His reputation for love, including both justice and

---

*When Manasseh did this and other kinds of abominations, he broke the covenant between God and Israel so seriously that the exile of his people was inevitable from that time on (2 Kings 23:26, 27; see Roy Gane, "The End of the Israelite Monarchy," *Journal of the Adventist Theological Society* 10 [1999]: 344, 345, 348–350).

mercy, is crucial because human beings are drawn to Him and the salvation that He offers only to the extent that His character draws them. If they see that His people are little different from everyone else and maybe worse in some ways (compare Judges 19 with Genesis 19), why should they expect that a covenant connection with Him will help them?

In Daniel 7 and 8, the little horn acts as an intruder that tries to get away with a hostile corporate takeover of God's covenant and the blessings that go with it. However, judgment by the heavenly court strips the dominion from this power and awards it to God's holy people (7:26, 27). God gives this prize to His people because they belong to Him. "The 'meek . . . will inherit the earth' (Matthew 5:5; cp. Psalm 37:11) for the same reason that Canaan was promised to Abraham: because they have a covenant relationship with Him."

Antichrist

In the sixteenth century, the Reformers concluded that the little horn symbolizes the Church of Rome. Counterreformers attempted to deflect this negative assessment of their church in either of two directions: Preterists said the little-horn prophecies were fulfilled before the church existed, in the time and person of Antiochus IV Epiphanes. And futurists shifted the fulfillment of these prophecies much later, to an "antichrist" that has not yet appeared. It didn't matter that the counterreformers' views were contradictory; they were effective distractions—just as in stories, some friends of the "bad guy" say he went that-a-way and point in one direction while others say, No, he went that-a-way and point in the opposite direction.

Preterism and futurism are mutually exclusive approaches. Neither of them matches the data in the biblical text. Regarding preterism, we have found that Antiochus IV Epiphanes doesn't adequately match the profile of the little horn: Although there are some similarities, Antiochus lived at the wrong time and place, and his career doesn't fit the scope of what the little horn was to do (see chapter 10).

Here are some major difficulties with the futurist view:

1. Daniel portrays the little horn as arising during the breakup of the Roman Empire, which occurred in the fifth century A.D.

From our perspective, this is history, not something yet future.

2. In Daniel 7, one power follows on the heels of another. There's no major gap between the prophesied empires and the little horn; it's contemporary with the other powers that follow Rome, as shown by the fact that several of them fall before the little horn during the time when it is rising.

3. Scripture indicates that Christianity has not been spared from an antichrist until some time in the future; it has already experienced an antichrist. First John 4 tells us what it means to be "antichrist": "By this you know the Spirit of God: every spirit that confesses that Jesus Christ has come in the flesh is from God; and every spirit that does not confess Jesus is not from God; and this is the spirit of the antichrist, of which you have heard that it is coming, and now it is already in the world" (verses 2, 3).

It isn't enough for us to believe that Jesus is human, or, on the other hand, that He is divine. It is crucial that we accept that He has come from God in the flesh—meaning that He is divine-human, because only if He has this combination can He serve as the bridge or ladder between fallen, mortal human beings and the pure, holy God (compare John 1:51). Only a divine-human Being can mediate as our royal Melchizedek high priest, who both has full access to God and "has been tempted in all things as we are, yet without sin" (Hebrews 4:15).

There is more than one way to be "antichrist." One can explicitly deny Jesus' divinity or His humanity. Or one can implicitly deny "that Jesus Christ has come in the flesh" by denying what His divine-human mission accomplished through setting up an ongoing earthly sacrifice in place of His "once-for-all" sacrifice (Hebrews 9:28) and setting up in place of His all-sufficient heavenly priesthood (Hebrews 4:14–16; 6:19–10:25) a human priesthood that blasphemously claims to forgive sins.

We have identified the little horn as the Church of Rome not out of some kind of prior prejudice but simply by following the evidence in the Bible and recognizing the remarkably accurate way in which Daniel's prophecies have been fulfilled. These predictions are clearly from God, who seeks to reveal His character and way of salvation through Christ, to warn us about spiritual danger, and to assure us that He will carry us through if we are faithful to Him.

In implicating the Church of Rome, the Bible has pointed out an institutional system of hierarchy, ritual, and dogma that is contrary to God. However, this by no means excludes all members of that church from ultimate salvation.[5] Jesus said, " 'I have other sheep, which are not of this fold; I must bring them also, and they shall hear My voice; and they shall become one flock with one shepherd' " (John 10:16; compare Revelation 18:4, where God calls His people from end-time "Babylon," Revelation's equivalent of Daniel's little horn). Through the centuries, many wonderful people have belonged to the Church of Rome. Their sincerity, spirituality, sacrificial living for Christ and unselfish service for others are a source of inspiration to all Christians. Would that we were all as devoted as was Mother Teresa, the Albanian nun who gave her life for the human dregs of Calcutta!

1. Roy Gane, *Altar Call* (Berrien Springs, Mich.: Diadem, 1999), 210–215; Roy Gane, *Leviticus, Numbers,* NIV Application Commentary (Grand Rapids: Zondervan, 2004), 281, 282, 366–368. For more detail, see Roy Gane, *Cult and Character: Purification Offerings, Day of Atonement, and Theodicy* (Winona Lake, Ind.: Eisenbrauns, 2005), 144–151, 154–156, 162, 294–299.

2. See Roy Gane, "Judgment as Covenant Review," *Journal of the Adventist Theological Society* 8 (1997): 190, 191.

3. Gane, "Judgment as Covenant Review," 191.

4. Compare William H. Shea, *Selected Studies on Prophetic Interpretation,* Daniel and Revelation Committee Series 1, Frank H. Holbrook, ed. (Silver Spring, Md.: Biblical Research Institute, 1992), 145; Gerhard Pfandl, *Daniel: The Seer of Babylon* (Hagerstown, Md.: Review and Herald, 2004), 80–82.

5. Pfandl, 82, 83.

Judged by Choosing the God Who Lets Us Choose

Human sin began when Eve accepted a misrepresentation of the character of God that suggested that He uses His authority to keep His created beings from realizing their full potential and that He does so because He wants to subordinate them to Himself. In other words, God is an unfair tyrant and His claim to be "love" (1 John 4:8) is hypocrisy. Then and now, the great war has always been over the character of God. This issue has shaped the conflict at every stage. Satan and his followers want God's position, and to get it, they challenge His justice as Absalom challenged the fairness of his father, King David (2 Samuel 15:2–6).

So, what will end the great war? God is mercifully waiting for people to change their minds and switch allegiance from Satan to Him. Many don't realize that there is a great war, let alone comprehend the nature of the two sides, their role, and the stakes involved.

Obviously, God can't ultimately help those hostages of Satan who don't admit that they are hostages and refuse to be rescued. God has based His government on love, which is His character and which is the only principle on which intelligent beings with free choice can harmoniously coexist in the universe and not destroy each other.[1] If God forced people to be saved, He would be denying love, which requires free choice. Love can never be forced, or it is not love. This is why God made humans with freedom to choose. C. S. Lewis explained: "Free will, though it makes evil possible, is also the only thing that makes possible any love or goodness or joy worth having."[2]

If all God wanted were control over us, He could have easily made us robots. But robots could never love Him, no matter how intricately He programmed their circuitry. So Jesus died to save us with our power of choice intact. On the one hand, God doesn't force everyone to be saved. But on the other, He doesn't want anyone to perish who can be saved by learning what is really going on (Ezekiel 33:11; 2 Peter 3:9).

Jesus predicted to His disciples, " 'This gospel of the kingdom shall be preached in the whole world for a witness to all the nations, and then the end shall come' " (Matthew 24:14). Notice the purpose of preaching the gospel: "for a witness to all the nations." A witness of what? In light of the rest of Jesus' teaching, we can see that the witness testifies to the loving character of God and His rule as revealed by what He has done and continues to do for us through Jesus Christ. Jesus didn't say that the end would come when everyone is converted. Rather, the end will come when everyone has had an *informed opportunity* to choose God, which is brought about by preaching.

The purpose of Christian preaching is not to glorify the preacher, entertain the crowd, fill a necessary slot in the worship service, make people feel secure without experiencing change in their lives, or generate numbers of baptisms that will impress the preacher's supervisors. The purpose of Christian preaching is to give witness to who God is and what He is really like so that people can clearly choose for or against Him. If Christians do this, they've preached the gospel. Evangelism is theodicy—justification of the character of God.

Preachers have the awesome privilege and responsibility of pointing people to Christ as the ultimate revelation of God's character. However, they're not responsible for the results any more than sentinels are responsible for what people do when they faithfully blow the warning trumpet (Ezekiel 33:1–9). It is Christ Himself, not the human preacher, who draws all people to Himself because He was lifted up on the cross (John 12:32)!

The "preaching" or "proclamation" of the gospel has a far broader meaning than formal public speaking to groups of people. We can proclaim the gospel in small groups or one to one, as when Jesus unfolded the good news of salvation to a leading Pharisee named Nicodemus (John 3) and a Samaritan woman by a well (John 4). "Preachers" are not limited to professional clergy. Every Christian— male or female, young or old—is a "minister" in a "royal priesthood" (1 Peter 2:9). Preaching is not even limited to speaking, as Francis of Assisi recognized when he urged, "Preach the gospel. Use words if you have to."

In Old Testament times, the ark of the covenant in the Israelite sanctuary contained the stone tablets of God's Ten Commandments. These served as the "testimony" or "witness" (Exodus 25:16, 21)—that is, the conditions or stipulations of the covenant between God and His chosen people. However, now that Christ's life, death on the cross, and resurrection have revealed God's character in a greater way than stone tablets ever could (2 Corinthians 3), it is the good news of His kingdom that is "a witness to all the nations."

Christian witness is not dry theory. The gospel is a story of an experience, a personal encounter with God. Witnesses tell what they have witnessed firsthand, not simply what they have heard from others or read in a book. That's why John, the beloved disciple, began his first letter to the Christian church this way: "What was from the beginning, what we have heard, what we have seen with our eyes, what we beheld and our hands handled, concerning the Word of Life . . . we proclaim to you" (1 John 1:1, 3).

Similarly, when Jesus cast a legion of evil spirits from a man, He told him to go home to his people and tell his own experience with God: " 'Report to them what great things the Lord has done for you, and how He had mercy on you' " (Mark 5:19). This is the most powerful witness that anyone in the universe can give. Only saved human beings, not even angels, can testify to the Lord's mercy by saying, "I once was lost, but now I'm found!" As a converted former prostitute from Wisconsin recently put it: "The last Man who bought me paid for me with His blood!"

Scope of the pre-Advent judgment

When God reveals His character, especially through the love He has shown in Christ, He gives people an opportunity to choose Him. Without this opportunity, the "ballot" would contain only one name: Satan. By adding His name to the ballot, God makes it a real "election" rather than a sham like the ones that dictators like Saddam Hussein have staged, in which they receive practically 100 percent of the vote because there are no other choices. And God gives everyone who "votes" for Him the privilege of living under His benevolent government rather than under the tyranny of Satan.

God doesn't force anyone to choose Him or to live for all eternity with Him. The choices He gives are real choices. When people choose Satan, they choose his government and they cast their fate with him, just as people from various nations who chose to adopt Nazism during World War II linked their fate with that of Adolf Hitler.

Since God is the ultimate Ruler of the universe, and since He alone is fair, He "tallies the votes" and allows all of His created beings to witness each stage of the "judgment" process so that they can be assured that He has done everything right. Perhaps we can compare these "cosmic monitors" to the international teams of U.N. observers who monitor elections in some countries to make sure that they are properly carried out.

The first stage of judgment (Daniel 7) takes place before Christ's second coming and determines whether people are saved or lost. Many Christians sincerely believe that God makes His judgment based on whether or not they've sinned. But this is a ridiculous idea because "all have sinned" (Romans 3:23). How could a judgment distinguish between two groups on this basis? It would be like deciding who gets to enjoy a free Caribbean cruise on the basis of who is breathing! When it comes to being sinners, we're all in a titanic mess, cruising to the bottom in the same sinking boat. The question in the judgment is not whether we've sinned, but whether we've accepted salvation through the sacrifice of Jesus Christ.

When Jesus forgave the woman caught in adultery, He said, " 'Neither do I condemn you; go your way. From now on sin no more' " (John 8:11). In doing so, He wiped out the condemnation she bore for her past life and gave her a new start. If she cherished this forgiveness, based on her new relationship to God, she wouldn't hop in bed with someone other than her husband. The judgment is based on the fact that her life after conversion would reveal whether or not she was faithful. If she subsequently rejected God and threw away the forgiveness she had received, her conversion would be ir-relevant and therefore her whole life—including her life before for-giveness—would condemn her (compare Ezekiel 18:24; Matthew 18:32–35).

So we see that for true believers, the pre-Advent judgment is con-cerned with our life after conversion. God shows whether we have continued to cherish the forgiveness we've received and have accept-ed the transformation that He offers. There's no point in the judg-ment considering the cases of the people who never had believed in God at some point or at least claimed some kind of belief because *the issue in the judgment is the postconversion life.* If there were no conversion or claim of conversion, there couldn't possibly be a post-conversion life to investigate. To use an analogy, a favorable court decision regarding a class-action lawsuit that benefits widows only helps women who have lived on after their husbands have died. Women who haven't had such a postmarried life are simply outside the scope of the judgment.

What Jesus told Nicodemus about salvation through Himself supports the idea that the pre-Advent judgment need not decide whether people who have never had a relationship with God will be saved or lost. He said that " 'whoever believes in him [Jesus] is not condemned, but whoever does not believe *stands condemned already* because he has not believed in the name of God's only begotten Son' " (John 3:18, NIV, margin; emphasis supplied). Those who be-lieve are released from condemnation because "the free gift of God is eternal life in Christ Jesus our Lord" (Romans 8:1; 6:23). By con-trast, those who don't believe and thereby reject the gift are already condemned because "the wages of sin is death" (verse 23).

This implies that the default position in which individual human beings initially find themselves is condemnation. Because "all have sinned and fall short of the glory of God" (Romans 3:23), there is only one way for anyone to be rescued from eternal death: " 'Believe in the Lord Jesus, and you shall be saved' " (Acts 16:31). " 'There is salvation in no one else; for there is no other name under heaven that has been given among men, by which we must be saved' " (Acts 4:12). Note that the words "no other name" don't mean that people who haven't literally heard the name of Jesus have no chance of be-ing saved. Christ "was the true light which, coming into the world, enlightens every man" (John 1:9)—including those who don't know Him by name and have no access to the Bible (compare Romans 2:14–16).

If you were on the *Titanic* when it struck an iceberg in the North Atlantic in 1912, you would surely have died unless you were able to get into a lifeboat. Your default position was to be lost at sea. If you'd been thrown into the icy water and then were invited into a lifeboat, it would have been suicide to refuse the invitation. Of course, we know the story: There weren't enough lifeboats, and those fortunate enough to get in let others perish rather than to risk overloading their lifeboats. Jesus is a much better lifeboat. He is big enough to invite and help all aboard who want to be saved.

Notice that I said that the default position in which *individual* human beings initially find themselves is to be lost. It is true that through Christ's sacrifice, God has already ensured that our world will be saved. But whether individuals will be part of that restored world depends on their choice to accept God's gift of salvation. This difference is clear in 2 Corinthians 5:18–20: "God [has] reconciled us to Himself through Christ, and gave us the ministry of reconciliation, namely, that God was in Christ reconciling the world to Himself, not counting their trespasses against them, and He has committed to us the word of reconciliation. Therefore, we are ambassadors for Christ, as though God were entreating through us; we beg you on behalf of Christ, be reconciled to God."

Paul's point here is that because God through Christ has already established reconciliation for the whole world in the sense of offering a general amnesty for all who have sinned against Him, those who have accepted God's offer are "ambassadors" for Him in the sense of inviting others to accept God's offer of reconciliation too.

Accepting God's offer of amnesty

Amnesty from God doesn't mean that at the Cross He automatically forgave and saved everybody. Both ancient and modern history have repeatedly shown that when a state or province belonging to a nation breaks away and declares independence, war often results. Reestablishing unity and peace requires reconciliation through putting away differences. If the "mother" nation is stronger (as in the American Civil War), it sets the terms. An effective way for it to regain the loyalty of as many rebels as possible is to offer amnesty to all of them who will end hostilities and lay down their weapons. While such amnesty is offered to a group, it always carries conditions, and its benefits only apply to those individuals who accept the conditions.

Former rebels who have experienced the benefits of rejoining the mother nation make the best "ambassadors" to rebels who are still fighting. For instance, Waheed Baghrani, thus far the highest-level Taliban commander to accept Afghanistan's offer of amnesty, said, "My message to those still fighting is they should take this golden chance and come back and build the country."[3] Similarly, Christians who enjoy peace with God (Romans 5:1) are ambassadors to people who are still at war with God. Our job is to tell them that the war is already won, the price of reconciliation has already been paid, and amnesty has already been extended to all who will simply accept it. This is the good news, the gospel.

When World War II ended in 1945, a Japanese soldier by the name of Schoichi Yokoi was hiding in the jungle on the Pacific island of Guam. He read a leaflet dropped from a United States aircraft that announced that the war was over, but he assumed it was a dirty trick to get him to surrender. He isolated himself from civilization, living in a primitive shelter and subsisting on whatever he could find in the jungle. When his clothes wore out, he made more clothing from the bark of trees. He lived in this state of stress and privation, thinking the war was still going on, until 1972—*twenty-seven years after the end of World War II.* Hunters found Yokoi while he was fishing and told him that his people had been enjoying peace for decades! Too bad the "ambassadors" didn't find him sooner!

When Jesus said " 'whoever believes in him is not condemned' " (John 3:18, NIV), He was speaking of judgment in the sense of condemnation. He didn't mean that the heavenly court won't judge the cases of believers in the sense of assessing them. Paul wrote, "We shall all stand before the judgment seat of God" (Romans 14:10) and "we must all appear before the judgment seat of Christ, that each one may be recompensed for his deeds in the body, according to what he has done, whether good or bad" (2 Corinthians

5:10). And Peter wrote, "It is time for judgment to begin with the household of God; and if it begins with us first, what will be the outcome for those who do not obey the gospel of God?" (1 Peter 4:17).

The scope of the pre-Advent judgment includes only those who've had at least a nominal connection with God.* Rebels who have never laid down their arms are automatically excluded from amnesty, but those who have regained friendly terms at some point, can claim the benefits of loyalty. The question is, are they really loyal as they say they are, or have they chosen to give up their loyalty? Because the gospel calls those who respond to "unconditional surrender" to God and loyalty to Him, a judgment is necessary to verify that they meet the condition.

Paul expressed the need for continuing loyalty: "Although you were formerly alienated and hostile in mind, engaged in evil deeds, yet He has now reconciled you in His fleshly body through death, in order to present you before Him holy and blameless and beyond reproach—if indeed you continue in the faith firmly established and steadfast, and not moved away from the hope of the gospel that you have heard, which was proclaimed in all creation under heaven, and of which I, Paul, was made a minister" (Colossians 1:21–23).

Assurance of salvation is based upon a present and continuing relationship with God through Christ. John said, "He who has the Son has life; he who does not have the Son of God does not have life" (1 John 5:12, NKJV). He didn't say that those who had Christ at some time in the past have life. Nor did he say that those who have Christ now will be automatically guaranteed life in the future even if they turn away from Christ.

---

*Compare Ellen G. White, *The Great Controversy Between Christ and Satan* (Nampa, Idaho: Pacific Press®, 1950), 480: "In the typical service only those who had come before God with confession and repentance, and whose sins, through the blood of the sin offering, were transferred to the sanctuary, had a part in the service of the Day of Atonement. So in the great day of final atonement and investigative judgment the only cases considered are those of the professed people of God. The judgment of the wicked is a distinct and separate work, and takes place at a later period."

Outcomes of the pre-Advent judgment

We've already found that in the pre-Advent judgment, God demonstrates whether people are saved or lost based on whether their postconversion lives show that they've continued to accept Him and His salvation and that He involves His created beings in this judgment process. On the ancient Day of Atonement, the sanctuary that represented God's administration and character was cleansed (Leviticus 16; 23:26–32). In the same way, the end-time judgment "justifies" the sanctuary (Daniel 8:14) by vindicating God's character as just when He distinguishes between the two opposing parties.* He acknowledges human choices toward Him by condemning the rebels and vindicating the loyal, whose sins are forgiven.

In what sense could a judgment be regarded as justifying God's sanctuary? Second Samuel 14 gives us an important hint. In this chapter, the woman of Tekoa implores King David to grant amnesty to her guilty son. She says, "Let the king and his throne be clean" (verse 9, my translation). David's throne stood for his administration, which involved his authority and justice. Similarly, God's place of enthronement—His sanctuary (Jeremiah 17:12)—represents His authority and His justice. David and his justice needed to be legally "clean." Likewise, God's justice must be vindicated.

Why does God's justice need vindication? For one thing, He and His sanctuary need vindication because of the defiantly rebellious sins of the little-horn power, which defame the Lord and pollute His sanctuary just as the Israelite sanctuary was defiled when God's people violated His worship system (Leviticus 20:3; Numbers 19:13, 20).

---

*" 'Cleansing/being pure' in Leviticus 16 and 'being just/righteous' in Daniel 8:14 refer to the same thing in two different ways. . . . In the contexts of Job 4:17, Leviticus 16, and Daniel 8:14, these words mean basically the same thing: legal cleansing or vindication" (Gane, 242, 243; compare Niels-Erik Andreasen, "Translation of *Nisdaq/Katharisthēsetai* in Daniel 8:14," in *Symposium on Daniel,* Daniel and Revelation Committee Series 2, Frank H. Holbrook, ed. [Silver Spring, Md.: Biblical Research Institute, 1986], 483–486; Richard M. Davidson, "The Meaning of Nis\daq in Daniel 8:14," *Journal of the Adventist Theological Society* 7 [1996]: 111, 112).

Second, God forgives truly guilty people, calls them holy, and gives the world to them (Daniel 7; 8). By forgiving such people, He raises questions about His justice. Compare the story of David and the woman of Tekoa: If the woman hadn't taken the blame, David as judge would have borne judicial responsibility and damaged his reputation for justice by letting a guilty person off the hook.[4]

Have you sinned and then experienced God's forgiveness? If so, you know what I'm talking about. God forgives truly guilty people, which a just judge is not supposed to do (compare Deuteronomy 25:1). But God does it anyway, based on the sacrifice of His Son, who paid the cost of mercy. God is just when He justifies people—but only those who genuinely believe in Jesus (Romans 3:26) as demonstrated in their life (Galatians 5:6; James 2:26). The judgment reveals whether or not this is so (Ecclesiastes 12:14).

1. Roy Gane, *Altar Call* (Berrien Springs, Mich.: Diadem, 1999), 269, 270.

2. *The New Encyclopedia of Christian Quotations,* Mark Water, ed. (Grand Rapids: Baker, 2000), 378.

3. Quoted in "Verbatim," Time (June 13, 2005), 11.

4. Gane, 233, 234; Roy Gane, *Leviticus, Numbers,* NIV Application Commentary (Grand Rapids: Zondervan, 2004), 284, 285. For more detail, see Roy Gane, *Cult and Character: Purification Offerings, Day of Atonement, and Theodicy* (Winona Lake, Ind.: Eisenbrauns, 2005), 318–323, 338–344.

The Relationship Between the Gospel and the Judgment

The ancient Day of Atonement involved a judgment between loyal and disloyal Israelites that foreshadowed the pre-Advent judgment. The loyal received moral cleansing (Leviticus 16:30), but the disloyal were condemned (23:29, 30).[1] Like the pre-Advent judgment, the scope of the Day of Atonement was restricted to God's people (see chapter 12). In this case, God's people were defined as the community of Israelites, who experienced the atoning benefit of the morning and evening burnt offerings (Numbers 28:1–8) that pointed forward to Christ's sacrifice.

Not all Israelites were loyal. Among them were those who had tasted the heavenly gift of deliverance from slavery and of manna in the wilderness but who ungratefully chose rebellion by sinning defiantly, by spurning God's gracious provision for restoration, and/or by refusing to show humble loyalty to God on the Day of Atonement by practicing self-denial and refraining from work (see Numbers 15:30, 31; Numbers 16; Leviticus 23:29, 30; compare Hebrews 6:4).

What people do demonstrates where their loyalty lies. Loyalty isn't simply an abstract concept distinct from actions. Is a man who cheats on his wife loyal? Is a politician who lies to the members of her district loyal? Is a "Christian" Bible teacher who undermines students' faith loyal? Of course not. We show our loyalty to God by our actions.

However, none of our loyal actions can save us. God saves us by His grace, which we receive as a gift through faith/trust in Him (Ephesians 2:8, 9). Nevertheless, faith necessarily produces loyal actions. Jesus forgave the woman caught in adultery, erasing her guilt. Then she was to cherish and live in harmony with the forgiveness she had received (John 8:11). God would hold her accountable only for her life after conversion.

Jesus takes us just as we are, but He doesn't leave us that way! James said, "Just as the body without the spirit is dead, so also faith without works is dead" (James 2:26). Living faith is active, outgoing, and unselfish—working through love, which is the basic principle of God's character and law (Galatians 5:6; 1 John 4:8; Matthew 22:37–40). Couch-potato faith that does nothing positive for anyone is dead. In fact, it is not effective faith at all, and without living faith, the salvation equation of *grace* + *faith* = *salvation* is broken. Faith is the human hand that grasps grace, the hand of God. But a dead human hand can't grasp anything.

When God told Abram (later Abraham) to leave his homeland for a country that He would show him, Abram announced to Sarah, his wife, and to his entire household that they were packing up and moving. So "Abram went forth as the LORD had spoken to him" (Genesis 12:4). Was that faith or works? Yes and Yes, because faith and works are inseparable.

The book of Ecclesiastes ends with the words, "God will bring every act to judgment, everything which is hidden, whether it is good or evil" (12:14). Earlier we mentioned the words of Paul: "We must all appear before the judgment seat of Christ, that each one may be recompensed for his deeds in the body, according to what he has done, whether good or bad" (2 Corinthians 5:10). How can God justly judge us on the basis of our works when we aren't saved by our works but rather are saved by grace through faith? The answer is that our works faithfully reveal the quality of our faith just as the quality of a house reveals the quality of the workmanship that produced it.

There's a story about two brilliant artists, one hard-working and one motivationally challenged. A king commissioned them to decorate a grand hallway in his palace; one artist was to paint the wall on one side of the hallway, and the other artist the wall on the other side. The king promised to pay them in gold at the end of the year.

The industrious artist began to paint right away and worked diligently all year. The other artist procrastinated until the week before the year was up, trusting that his genius would enable him to do the job in a short time. When at last he went into the hallway, he discovered to his horror that his colleague had wrought such magnificently intricate art that there was no way he could match it in the time he had left. So he covered his side of the hallway with mirrors to reflect the other man's work.

Then the king came to inspect the hallway. He looked with pleasure and admiration on the work of the industrious artist, congratulated him warmly, and directed his servants to bring bags of glittering gold to pay the man. Then the king turned to leave. Alarmed, the lazy artist asked, "But Your Highness, where is *my* payment?" The king pointed to the reflection of the gold in the mirrors the artist had installed and replied, "There!" The quality of work that he had chosen to produce revealed his character and determined his reward.

Someone might object, "God can read our minds (Genesis 6:5; Psalm 139:23; Matthew 12:24, 25; Luke 7:39, 40). Why doesn't He judge us by our thoughts of faith rather than by our works?"

He doesn't because the judgment is not for God's information but to inform His created beings, who don't know everything and can't read thoughts![2] In a courtroom, would it make sense to introduce as Exhibit A a piece of evidence that the jury couldn't see? So the final judgment, produced for the benefit of the inhabitants of the universe, must present evidence that they can perceive.

How God judges us

If we are saved by grace through faith/trust in God that results in works, does this mean that we contribute to our own salvation? No. Ephesians 2:8 says, "By grace you have been saved *through* faith; *and that not of yourselves,* it is the gift of God" (emphasis supplied). Of ourselves, we do not possess sufficient faith to be saved. We can only cry out to God, "Lord, I believe; help my unbelief!" (see Mark 9:24, NKJV). Neither can we repent by ourselves. Repentance is a gift from God (Acts 5:31; 2 Timothy 2:25). Even obedience to God is a gift because God pours His love, the basis of His law, into our hearts through His Holy Spirit (Romans 5:5).

If everything we need for salvation is a gift, on what basis can God judge us? We are so accustomed to assessment on the basis of our own performance, whether in school, sports, music, or work, that we tend to think that God must also judge our performance. We have trouble getting it through our thick skulls that God really judges us on *how we receive His gift!* It is not about what we do for Him, but what we let Him do for us. "We are saved by grace and grace alone. But when we are saved by grace, we do works that God accepts as good. So, you see, when God judges us by our works, He is simply judging whether or not we have received His grace as the power to do good works. If we are saved by God's grace, our works will be good works. If we are not saved by God's grace, our works will be sinful works. That's why God judges us by our works."[3]

The virgin Mary got it right when the angel Gabriel told her she would give birth to the Messiah. She replied, " 'Behold the maidservant of the Lord! Let it be to me according to your word' " (Luke 1:38, NKJV). She simply said Yes to God, letting Him do with her as He wished—letting Him physically plant Christ in her womb through His Holy Spirit (verse 35). We experience something similar spiritually: If we say Yes to God, Christ and His love will come into our minds and hearts through the Holy Spirit (John 14:15–20, 23; Romans 5:5; 8:9, 10; Galatians 2:20; Colossians 1:27; Revelation 3:20), who gives us spiritual rebirth (John 3:3–8).[4]

Transformation

How different this "God possession" is from demon possession! Witches gain power by inviting demons into their bodies. The more powerful the demons, the more power the witches possess . . . and the more powerfully and dangerously they are enslaved by Satan and his foul, fallen angels—who are selfish and cruel and don't respect human free choice.[5] "God possession" is just as real as demon possession, even though most Christians don't treat it as real. But we don't have mere angels—even unfallen ones—living in us. Rather, we invite the God of the universe, our Creator, to come into us. Is that power or what! When Christ and the Holy Spirit dwell in us, we need have absolutely no fear of ultimate danger from the comparatively feeble powers of darkness (Romans 8:31–39).

"God possession" doesn't mean that we have power that accords with earthly standards of wealth, fame, and the ability to force others to do our will. Nor does it necessarily mean that we are immune from all physical harm, so that bullets coming our way always fall to the ground around us. God doesn't control us by bypassing our ability to choose what we do, although under special circumstances He has shown Himself capable of doing that to some stubborn individuals (see, for example, Numbers 24; 1 Samuel 19:23, 24). But He does give people courage and the ability to do wonderful things that they wouldn't otherwise do (see the books of Judges and Acts). Above all, He provides His kind of love, which is the most powerful force in the universe and is the opposite of the selfishness that governs Satan, his filthy demons, and those they possess. Christians have suffered catastrophic loss by grossly underestimating what God wants to do for, in, and through them.

One of the most powerful expressions of how God wants to change us for the better is in Titus 3:4–7: "When the kindness of God our Savior and His love for mankind appeared, He saved us, not on the basis of deeds which we have done in righteousness, but according to His mercy, by the washing of regeneration and renewing by the Holy Spirit, whom He poured out upon us richly through Jesus Christ our Savior, that being justified by His grace we might be made heirs according to the hope of eternal life."

Who saved us?

God.

Why?

Not because of any righteous deeds that we have done, but because He loves us.

How has He saved us?

By mercifully giving us rebirth and renewal by the Holy Spirit, who is richly available to us because of Christ.

Having received this rebirth and renewal, we have been justified—in other words, made righteous—by His grace. So "the washing of regeneration and renewing by the Holy Spirit" is the same experience as "being justified by His grace," by which we are heirs of eternal life.[6]

Of course, this experience includes legal freedom from condemnation for our sins (Romans 8:1). But it involves much more as well:

transformation from the inside out through the indwelling Christ and Holy Spirit! God doesn't merely declare us righteous as a kind of legal fiction. Rather, He makes us righteous and declares us what He makes us. We cannot separate His declaration from the transformation He accomplishes.[7] Remember that in the beginning, when God spoke, it was so!

Interestingly, in the Hebrew Bible, certain verbs that mean "create" (root *br'*) and "forgive" (root *slh*) are used only in connection with what God does. Human beings can create in the sense that they make things, but they always make them out of something else. God, on the other hand, can make things out of nothing (Hebrews 11:3). Human beings can forgive the wrongs they do to each other. God, on the other hand, has a special kind of forgiveness that not only gives up a "debt" but also provides positive restoration and transformation by His re-creative power. Ellen G. White was right on target when she observed: "Forgiveness has a broader meaning than many suppose. . . . God's forgiveness is not merely a judicial act by which He sets us free from condemnation. It is not only forgiveness *for* sin, but reclaiming *from* sin. It is the outflow of redeeming love that transforms the heart. David had the true conception of forgiveness when he prayed, 'Create in me a clean heart, O God; and renew a right spirit within me.' Psalm 51:10."[8]

Now we are ready to understand a profound prophecy pointing forward to Christ and what He would accomplish for us as God's suffering "servant." Translated quite literally, Isaiah 53:11 reads, "My servant shall make righteous a righteous person for many" (my translation). This is language of judgment. Compare Deuteronomy 25:1 and 1 Kings 8:32, where a just judge "makes" righteous the righteous or "makes" wicked the wicked—that is, the judge vindicates or condemns according to the reality of a person's character. To do otherwise is unjust (Proverbs 17:15; Isaiah 5:23).

Isaiah 53:11 says that God's servant vindicates many people. On what basis? The next words answer: "He will bear their iniquities." Does that make them righteous? Yes, or He would not be just in vindicating them. God says, "I do not make righteous the wicked" (Exodus 23:7, my translation).

Christ's sacrifice shows God to be just when He justifies those who have faith in Jesus (Romans 3:25, 26). Why? This sacrifice, received by faith, makes a person righteous so that he or she can justly be judged righteous. This is not legal fiction but instead transformation of both character and standing by divine grace. Not that newly "righteous" people are instantly perfect, but that they now pledge allegiance to the Lord and receive His renewing Spirit (Titus 3:4–7; Romans 5:5).

As Christians, all of our good, loyal works are part of receiving God's gift. But if our salvation is totally a gift, why then do we struggle? Here are three reasons. First, we are contending with sin, Satan, and the distractions of this life, which lure us from our loyalty to God (see Matthew 13:19–22). Being sober and vigilant "because your adversary the devil walks about like a roaring lion, seeking whom he may devour" requires constant attention (1 Peter 5:8, NKJV).

Second, it is hard for proud, self-sufficient people to accept a gift—to say, "Yes, I need help." Wives, here's why your husbands would rather drive around for hours than take a moment to stop and ask someone for directions, or why they would rather blunder unhappily through their marriage for decades rather than spend a few hours with a trained Christian counselor!

Third, receiving a gift can require work. A couple of years ago, my parents gave me their 1987 Mercury Cougar, for which I was deeply grateful. Getting it from California to my home in Michigan and maintaining it have taken some time and effort, but it was still a gift. Receiving from God the gift of a strong, pure, loving character requires cooperation on our part as we are refined through the difficulties of life. This is why Paul could say, "We also exult in our tribulations, knowing that tribulation brings about perseverance; and perseverance, proven character; and proven character, hope" (Romans 5:3, 4).

Judgment versus gospel assurance?

Some people say that the idea of a pre-Advent judgment wipes out the gospel assurance of salvation that Christians should enjoy. Dale Ratzlaff has written a book titled *The Cultic Doctrine of Seventh-day Adventists*. His book opposes the concept of an investigative judgment in the heavenly sanctuary before Christ's second coming. In it, Ratzlaff contrasts "teachings of the investigative judgment" (left column below) with his own evangelical view, which he calls "teachings of Scripture" (right column below).[9] There is no question that the latter category contains truth, but it is partial truth that fits with the "teachings of the investigative judgment" in the larger biblical picture rather than opposing these teachings as Ratzlaff claims.* We can confirm and enrich our understanding of the relationship between the gospel and the judgment by briefly answering each of the "contrasts," which Ratzlaff has conveniently summarized in a table. His "contrasts" appear in the boxes and bold type below. My responses follow in lightface type.

Teachings of the investigative judgment:	Teachings of Scripture:
Sin-laden blood pollutes	**Blood cleanses**

Ratzlaff objects to the teaching that when Christ, our High Priest, applies His own sacrificial blood to cleanse us from sin, His blood becomes the means of transferring our sins to the heavenly sanctuary, with the result that the sanctuary must be cleansed through a pre-Advent judgment. Ratzlaff thinks that this idea casts disrepute upon Christ's blood by saying that it pollutes. However, sacrificial blood *itself* does not pollute. Rather, it *carries away* pollution from people when it is used for cleansing them, so that what receives it (including the sanctuary) also receives the impurity that it carries (Leviticus 6:27, 28).[10] Compare the way bathwater carries

---

*Compare Clifford Goldstein's critique of Ratzlaff's book, titled *Graffiti in the Holy of Holies* (Nampa, Idaho: Pacific Press®, 2003). I wrote my book *Altar Call* (Berrien Springs, Mich.: Diadem, 1999) partly to answer Ratzlaff's objections to the pre-Advent judgment, but I didn't mention by name him or anyone else to whom I was responding. There is a place for published debates and reviews that specifically refer to authors and hold them accountable for what they write in order to sharpen and advance our collective understanding. However, in Altar Call, my goal was to help the reader focus on the Lord of the sanctuary and fall in love with Him—an approach that ultimately supports our sanctuary teaching in the most powerful way.

dirt from the body and the way blood acts as an agent in the body to carry away waste products. There is nothing wrong with the water or blood. They are just doing their job!

Sins blotted out after 1844	Sins blotted out at repentance

Sins are removed through a two-phased process of atonement: (1) Upon repentance, *forgiveness* removes sin from the sinner (Leviticus 4:26, 31), and (2) the cleansing of the sanctuary on the Day of Atonement results in final *cleansing* for God's people (Leviticus 16:30; compare 1 John 1:9; Jeremiah 31:34). Before sin is finally cleansed or blotted out—that is, made eternally irrelevant—failure to live in harmony with the forgiveness that one has received can lead to forfeiting that forgiveness (Matthew 18:23–35).

Keep in mind that God's pre-Advent judgment, the end-time reality to which the Day of Atonement pointed, has to do with one's life after conversion, which God empowers (see John 8:11). The judgment is not meant to determine who has sinned, because all have sinned (Romans 3:23). Rather, it is about who is forgiven—present tense: "is and remains," not "was"!

If we allow God's grace to continue working in our lives, the judgment reaffirms our forgiveness and sets our assurance in concrete by making our sins eternally irrelevant. Remember that on the Day of Atonement, the high priest applied blood in the very places where it was applied throughout the year—thereby affirming the forgiveness that the Israelites had already received (Leviticus 16:16, 18, 19; compare 4:6, 7, 17, 18, 25, 30, 34).

Emphasis on personal works	Emphasis on faith in Christ

We are saved by grace through faith in Christ (Ephesians 2:8, 9), and this saving, new-covenant relationship results in works of love because God writes His law of love on our hearts through His Spirit (Galatians 5:6; Jeremiah 31:31–34, compare Matthew 22:36–40; Romans 5:5). The lack of works of love is a symptom that faith is dead (James 2:26), which means that the person hasn't accepted

111

God's saving grace. Works don't save us, but we aren't saved without the works that result from accepting God's gift of salvation. The horse that provides the power (grace) must be in front of the cart (works), but the cart must be there too. So it would be misleading to say that works have nothing to do with our salvation. The judgment deals with works as evidence for faith because the judgment is carried out for the benefit of God's created beings, who can't read thoughts of faith (Psalm 62:12; Ecclesiastes 12:14; Matthew 16:27; 1 Peter 1:17; Revelation 20:12; 22:12; compare Daniel 7:10).

Must achieve personal perfection of character	Must trust in Christ's sinless perfection

Christ is our blameless Sin Bearer, example, and sympathetic High Priest (1 Peter 2:21–25; Philippians 2:5–8; Hebrews 4:14–16). He takes away the condemnation that is ours because of past sin and transforms our lives through His Spirit (John 3:3–17; 8:11; Titus 3:4–7). Just as the Lord asked Abraham to "be blameless" (Genesis 17:1), Christ makes His people blameless (Ephesians 5:25–30; Revelation 14:5; 19:7, 8). It is His work to make us blameless. Our part is to be loyal (Leviticus 23:27–32; Revelation 14:12), wholeheartedly following the Lord wherever He leads (Numbers 14:24) and accepting what He wants to do with us (Luke 1:38). God's judgment simply accepts the decisions of people to be the kind of people they have chosen to be (Revelation 22:11).

Judgment deals with God's people	Judgment deals with the wicked

The ancient Day of Atonement dealt with the nominal, professed people of God—that is, the Israelites, cleansing the sins of those who remained loyal (Leviticus 16:29, 30) and condemning those who were disloyal (Leviticus 23:27–32). Similarly, the end-time judgment that vindicates God's justice as represented by the cleansing of His sanctuary is concerned with the nominal people of God—those who are at least called "Christians." This judgment benefits the "holy ones of the Most High" (Daniel 7:22, 27,

112

NRSV) and condemns the apostate little-horn power (Daniel 7:11, 26; 8:25), which we have identified with a professedly "Christian" organization. The pre-Advent judgment does not assess with the "wicked" in general who have had no connection to the Lord.

The atonement was not complete at the Cross	The atonement was complete at the Cross

The atonement was complete at the Cross in the sense that Christ's one and only atoning sacrificial death made complete *provision* for the salvation of all human beings (Hebrews 9:28; compare Romans 5:12–17). However, in order to receive the benefit of atonement, each individual must accept Christ by faith (John 3:16–18; Ephesians 2:8, 9). Atonement is relational reconciliation. So the process of atonement continues as long as we are being reconciled to God. Decades after Christ died on the cross, Paul appealed to the Corinthians to "be reconciled to God" (2 Corinthians 5:20), and his appeal is for us today as well.[11]

Christ's priestly mediation is a necessary work of atonement (Hebrews 9:11–15, compare Leviticus 4:31); and so is His Day of *Atonement* judgment ministry (Daniel 8:14; Leviticus 16—Day of *Atonement*). But we should remember that all atonement, including that of the end-time judgment, flows from Christ's once-for-all sacrificial death (see Leviticus 16:11, 15; Revelation 5:6).

Christ has a standing, pleading ministry	Christ has a seated, victorious ministry

Both are true. Since His ascension, Christ has been victorious and free to sit down with His Father (Hebrews 1:3). He can stand up if the situation calls for it (Acts 7:56). He can walk around as Mediator, meeting the needs of churches on earth (Revelation 1:12–20). As our Mediator, He can also stand to plead as our Defense Attorney because He carries the Cross event with Him (Revelation 5:6). His "pleading" isn't subservient begging. Rather, it is more like

113

legal pleading in a court situation, as in "How do you plead?" In Christ's case, His pleading is a triumphant demonstration of the evidence for His sacrifice, which makes it possible for Him to save those who accept what He has done for them.

1. Roy Gane, *Leviticus, Numbers,* NIV Application Commentary (Grand Rapids: Zondervan, 2004), 408, 409; Roy Gane, *Cult and Character: Purification Offerings, Day of Atonement, and Theodicy* (Winona Lake, Ind.: Eisenbrauns, 2005), 305–323.

2. Compare John T. Anderson, *Investigating the Judgment* (Hagerstown, Md.: Review and Herald, 2003), 44–46.

3. Erwin R. Gane, *Jesus Only: Paul's Letter to the Romans* (Roseville, Calif.: Amazing Facts, 2005), 48.

4. See ibid., 123, n. 1.

5. Rebecca Brown, *He Came to Set the Captives Free* (New Kensington, Penn.: Whitaker House, 1992), especially 45–47, 62.

6. E. R. Gane, 29, 32, 33, n. 3.

7. See ibid., 70.

8. Ellen G. White, *Thoughts From the Mount of Blessing* (Nampa, Idaho: Pacific Press®, 1955), 114.

9. Dale Ratzlaff, *The Cultic Doctrine of Seventh-Day Adventists* (Sedona, Ariz.: Life Assurance Ministries, 1996), 223.

10. See Roy Gane, *Altar Call* (Berrien Springs, Mich.: Diadem, 1999), 206, 207; Gane, *Leviticus, Numbers,* 148–150. For more detail, see R. Gane, *Cult and Character,* 165–180.

11. See further in Gane, *Altar Call,* 123–127.

CHAPTER

How God's Judgment Makes a Difference

You can't live in a war zone and escape the impact of war. From people who have survived armed conflicts in places like Rwanda, Kosovo, and Iraq, we learn that danger produces fear, suffering, and sorrow. It also gobbles up time, energy, and resources that could be used for other things. Even apart from the terrible toll war takes in deaths and injuries, it's expensive physically, emotionally, and economically. "Every gun that is made, every warship launched, every rocket fired signifies in the final sense, a theft from those who hunger and are not fed, those who are cold and are not clothed. This world in arms is not spending money alone. It is spending the sweat of its laborers, the genius of its scientists, the hopes of its children. This is not a way of life at all in any true sense. Under the clouds of war, it is humanity hanging on a cross of iron" (Dwight Eisenhower, April 16, 1953[1]).

But what if you know that help is on the way? That the liberation force has won the decisive victory? That the war is nearly over? That while you're still in a war zone, peace is coming soon—D-Day is in the past, and V-Day is almost here? Your discouragement and resignation would turn to hope and energy. You'd prepare to greet and cooperate with those who are about to liberate you.

This is where we are in the great war. Christ has won the decisive victory at the Cross, and He's in the final stage of completely liberating the world: the pre-Advent judgment! By the end of the judgment, which can come at any time, His people will be confirmed as His (see

115

Revelation 7:3, 4—the sealing). The next thing that happens will be His second coming. Rather than burning with legalistic zeal to try to save ourselves, which is hopeless and suicidal, we can be filled with joyful anticipation as we prepare to greet our conquering Savior. It is time to " 'lift up your heads, because your redemption is drawing near' " (Luke 21:28). "He will swallow up death for all time, and the Lord God will wipe tears away from all faces, and He will remove the reproach of His people from all the earth; for the Lord has spoken. And it will be said in that day, 'Behold, this is our God for whom we have waited that He might save us. This is the Lord for whom we have waited; let us rejoice and be glad in His salvation' " (Isaiah 25:8, 9).

Many liberators send advance agents to help prepare the way before the final assault begins. First go the scouts to assess the situation, relay military intelligence to help commanders decide on the most effective strategies, and coordinate with local people who have been engaged in covert resistance to the enemy. Then the commanders send air strikes and paratroops to soften up the enemy and spearhead the initial attack, after which the tanks go rolling in. So the invasion is a process that begins well before the onset of the final battle.

Again, that's where we are. God knows the situation, so He doesn't need spies to inform Him about what's going on. But He's sent His heavenly agents—the Holy Spirit and angels—to teach, equip, and empower us, the local people, to cooperate with Him in making His conquest as effective as possible. Only, in this war, effectiveness is not defined as the highest body count possible in the shortest possible time. To the contrary, it is defined as saving as many people as possible from the overwhelming destruction that Satan and his allies will soon experience.

To an extent, the situation we have been describing has been true throughout the Christian era. However, the fact that we are now living in the final period when " 'the hour of His judgment has come' " (Revelation 14:7) gives us a tremendous sense of urgency because there is so little time left for our fellow human beings to change their allegiance from "beastly" human and satanic power (Revelation 13) to their Creator and Savior, the King of the universe.

If we really believe that "the hour of His judgment has come," we will " 'fear God, and give Him glory . . . and worship Him who made the heaven and the earth and sea and springs of waters' " (Revelation

14:7). If we really believe it, we will keep the commandments of God and hold fast to our faith in Jesus (verse 12). If we really believe it, we will come out of the apostate, worldly, oppressive, end-time "Babylon" power that is opposed to God as ancient Babylon, Media-Persia, Greece, and Rome were (Revelation 18:4; compare 14:8).[2]

If we really believe that "the hour of His judgment has come," our priorities, goals, and courses of action will differ radically from those of other people, including lukewarm, Laodicean Christians (Revelation 3:14–21)—who are fixated on temporal security, materialism, and earthly gratification. We won't invest all our energies into piling up dollars, pesos, euros, dinars, or yen and the classy things that they can buy. We won't become assimilated into the secular, humanistic culture of contemporary society that drowns out the "still, small voice" of the Holy Spirit. We'll dare to be different—like Daniel, whose loyalty to God was so strong that empires couldn't shake it!

"The accuser of our brethren"

Revelation 12:10–12 has special meaning for us today, who live during the pre-Advent judgment: "I heard a loud voice in heaven, saying, 'Now the salvation, and the power, and the kingdom of our God and the authority of His Christ have come, for the accuser of our brethren has been thrown down, who accuses them before our God day and night. And they overcame him because of the blood of the Lamb and because of the word of their testimony, and they did not love their life even to death. For this reason, rejoice, O heavens and you who dwell in them. Woe to the earth and the sea, because the devil has come down to you, having great wrath, knowing that he has only a short time.' "

It is true that Satan was already the accuser of God's people in ancient times (Job 1; 2; Zechariah 3). It is also true that when Christ was on earth, He cast Satan down by defeating his demons through His ministry and that of His disciples (Luke 10:18) and above all by dying on the cross to reclaim the world (John 12:31, 32). However, there is a special sense in which the pre-Advent judgment throws down " 'the accuser of our brethren . . . who accuses them before our God day and night' " (Revelation 12:10).

The purpose of the pre-Advent judgment is precisely to vindicate God against the accusations of Satan and his cohorts. They charge that God is unfair when He saves some but not others (see chapters 4 and 12 of the present book). And Satan is particularly enraged that those who accept Christ will not share his ultimate fate in the lake of fire (Revelation 20). Every individual who is saved is a victory for God, whom Satan hates. So Satan is "the accuser of our brethren"—that is, of our brothers and sisters who are loyal to God. To deprive God of their company, Satan says that because they have sinned, they deserve eternal death. The great war ends with the same issue that Satan questioned at its beginning: the character of God.

Don't miss the following crucial points:

1. It is Satan, not God, who is trying to take away our assurance of salvation. In his attempt to destroy people, he tempts them to sin and then accuses them regarding those very sins. The legal term for gaining people's condemnation by luring them to commit a wrong is *entrapment.*

2. The pre-Advent judgment confirms the assurance of salvation of those who are loyal to God, confounding Satan's accusations. Those who are raising shrill protestations that the pre-Advent judgment teaching destroys a true Christian's gospel assurance are seeing the situation completely backwards. The only ones who find the judgment threatening are those who are disloyal to God.

3. It's no wonder that we see Satan today " 'having great wrath, knowing that he has only a short time' " (Revelation 12:12). Most of the Christian world doesn't understand or accept the pre-Advent judgment, but Satan does! In an intellectual sense, he is a better theologian than most human theologians, even though he's on the wrong side of theology.

4. People who are totally committed to God are victorious over Satan " 'because of the blood of the Lamb and because of the word of their testimony, and they did not love their life even to death' " (Revelation 12:11). Revelation 12:17 refers also to their loyalty and the basis of their victory: "The dragon was enraged with the woman, and went off to make war with the rest of her offspring, who keep the commandments of God and hold to the testimony of Jesus." This verse describes faithful followers of Christ throughout the Christian era, but it has special meaning during the time of the pre-Advent judgment, when those who persevere in their loyalty to God "keep the commandments of God and their faith in Jesus" (Revelation 14:12).

Confidence, rather than denial[3]

Many Christians are in a state of denial about the judgment because they fear it. A state of denial is a fascinating and dangerous psychological phenomenon. Since the destruction of the World Trade Center in New York City on September 11, 2001, a National Institute of Standards and Technology study has investigated the ability of people to evacuate when there is imminent danger. The intent was to make warning and rescue operations more successful in the future. A major problem is that it takes time for the reality of danger to sink into people's consciousness, even when the danger is obvious.

When the plane hit Elia Zedeño's building on 9/11, the effect was not subtle. From the 73rd floor of Tower 1, she heard a booming explosion and felt the building actually lurch to the south, as if it might topple. It had never done that before, even in 1993 when a bomb exploded in the basement, trapping her in an elevator. This time, Zedeño grabbed her desk and held on, lifting her feet off the floor. Then she shouted, "What's happening?"

You might expect that her next instinct was to flee. But she had the opposite reaction. "What I really wanted was for someone to scream back, 'Everything is OK! Don't worry. It's in your head.' "

She didn't know it at the time, but all around her, others were filled with the same reflexive incredulity. And the reaction was not unique to 9/11. Whether they're in shipwrecks, hurricanes, plane crashes, or burning buildings, people in peril experience remarkably similar stages. And the first one—even in the face of clear and urgent danger—is almost always a period of intense disbelief.[4]

Elia made it out of the building in time because one of her co-workers responded differently and yelled for her and others to get out. But many others in the twin towers lingered too long and perished. "At least 135 people who theoretically had access to open stairwells—and enough time to use them—never made it out."[5]

We badly want our comfortable status quo to continue; we hesitate to give it up until we are compelled to. Sometimes warnings come from God rather than from our physical senses or from other human beings. Angels warned Lot and his family, but they were in a state of denial and didn't want to leave their comfortable home. The angels had to drag them from Sodom, getting them out just before divine fire incinerated the city. Even then, Lot's wife disobeyed by looking back, and instantly she became a pillar of salt (Genesis 19). Her state of denial was lethal. The fact that she didn't treat the danger as real didn't diminish its reality.

Christians fear the judgment in part because it not only delivers those who are loyal to God but also condemns the disloyal (Hebrews 10:26–31). But a state of denial won't make the judgment go away. As with any other situation that involves life-and-death consequences—in this case, eternal life versus eternal death—the only sensible thing to do is to face it head on, assessing the options and their consequences. To do nothing is to choose death by default, just as those who lingered in the twin towers thereby determined their fate.

Yes, the scenario looks grim indeed for those who turn away from God. But God wants to save them, so He gives them fair warning. During the pre-Advent judgment, the warning goes like this: " 'If anyone worships the beast and his image, and receives a mark on his forehead or upon his hand, he also will drink of the wine of the wrath of God, which is mixed in full strength in the cup of His anger; and he will be tormented with fire and brimstone in the presence of the holy angels and in the presence of the Lamb. And the smoke of their torment goes up forever and ever; and they have no rest day and night, those who worship the beast and his image, and whoever receives the mark of his name' " (Revelation 14:9–11).

Why would God be so cruel as to give a warning like this? Actually, in giving this warning, God isn't being cruel—He's being merciful. He's letting people know the terrible consequences so that they can choose to avoid them. Suppose Allied planes had dropped leaflets on Hiroshima on August 5, 1945, warning everyone to leave the area because an atomic bomb would be dropped the next day. Would that have been cruel or kind? So if you've been in the wrong place in your relationship with God, please read His "leaflet," the Bible, and do something about your relationship. Don't just stand or sit there until all hell breaks loose!

For those who choose loyalty to God, the pre-Advent judgment is a different story. It's "about mercy and its results for us and for our divine King and Judge, who is also our Father. When we enter the judgment cherishing the forgiveness that we have already received, the judgment sets our confidence in concrete."[6]

Bible answers to our fears

The Bible answers our fears by informing us about the judgment so we can make an informed choice based on real data rather than sinking into self-denial or catapulting into overreaction. Here are the major factors:

1. We are judged by our works (Ecclesiastes 12:14; compare Daniel 7:10). That sounds scary because God knows everything. However, our deeds are only symptoms of our faith in the grace of God through which He saves us (Ephesians 2:8, 9; James 2:26). Since it is God who empowers our works through faith (Romans 5:5; Galatians 5:6; Philippians 2:12, 13), there is no room for legalism or despair, which are really two sides of the same miserable coin that vainly tries to buy God's favor rather than exulting in His grace.

2. Forgiveness that we have previously received can be rendered null and void in the judgment (see Ezekiel 18:24; Matthew 18:32–35). However, this can happen only if we sever our covenant connection with God by walking away from Him and barring Him from continuing to give us the transformation of character that is part of His forgiveness package (Hebrews 6:4–6). While we accept the change that He offers, we enjoy total assurance that our sins are forgiven (Romans 8:1–17; Colossians 1:21–23).

3. The judgment takes place in heaven, and we don't know when our cases will be considered. These factors can cause fear because they mean we can't clean up our act just in time for our court appearance. But God is interested in genuine, permanent commitment rather than hypocritical show that makes a temporary good impression but is not based on deep reality. Would you want to marry someone whom you saw only in a tuxedo or evening gown, without knowing what he or she looked and acted like during the ups and downs of ordinary life? Although we don't know when our individual cases come up, God has told us when the judgment as a whole began (A.D. 1844—see chapter 8 of the present book). He's also told

us what He wants us to do during this entire time: "Keep the commandments of God and hold fast to the faith of Jesus" (Revelation 14:12, NRSV).

Jesus said that God the Father " 'has given all judgment to the Son' " (John 5:22). Think about the implications of this statement. The Father does not judge any human being directly but depends on the judgment of His Son, Jesus Christ, who died to save you. People who invest in something or someone want to protect their investment. Dying for someone is the ultimate investment. But Jesus did more than die for you—He died the equivalent of the second death for you. He has more invested in you than anyone else in the universe possibly could have. Doesn't it make sense then that He would have a supreme interest in saving you if He possibly can—that is, if you let Him?

Not only has God loved you enough to send His own Son to die for you, but the Son Himself has lived on planet Earth for thirty-three years among faulty human beings like you and me. So He has experienced our weaknesses in a way that He never could have by mere observation. He's felt our sorrows, our pain, and our sicknesses (see Isaiah 53:3, 4). Although He never committed a sin, He "has been tempted in all things as we are" (Hebrews 4:15). So He is eminently qualified to serve as our merciful High Priest and Judge.

The role of a priest is to intercede, to mediate on someone's behalf. The fact that Christ is our High Priest and therefore our Mediator or Defense Attorney (see 1 John 2:1, our "Advocate") and at the same time our Judge (John 5:22) and " 'the faithful and true Witness' " (Revelation 3:14), should give us tremendous assurance. And there's more! "Jesus is also, by substitution, the accused, having voluntarily taken our place. Through the miracle of divine grace, Christ stands in our stead. 'For He made Him who knew no sin to be sin for us, that we might become the righteousness of God in Him' (2 Corinthians 5:21)."[7]

If we are with Jesus, everything is stacked in our favor and we have nothing to fear! Everything depends on our relationship to Jesus, who said: " 'Everyone therefore who shall confess Me before men, I will also confess him before My Father who is in heaven. But whoever shall deny Me before men, I will also deny him before My Father who is in heaven' " (Matthew 10:32, 33).

What greater "character reference" could you have than one from Jesus Christ?

Christians can enjoy five kinds of confidence during the pre-Advent judgment: (1) Confidence of access to God as Jesus, our High Priest, is ministering in the heavenly Holy of Holies (Hebrews 4:14–16). (2) Confidence that God is fair (Psalm 96). (3) Confidence that He will deliver from oppression (Daniel 7:21, 22, 26, 27; Psalm 9:1–4). (4) Confidence in the imminence of Christ's second coming (Daniel 8:14; Revelation 14:6, 7; compare Habakkuk 2:3; Amos 4:12). And (5) confidence that we are in a saved relationship with God (Psalm 50:3–6; 1 John 5:13).

Participation and commitment

On the ancient Day of Atonement, the Israelites could not physically see their high priest as he entered the sanctuary to purge it from their sins. Nevertheless, they were to participate in this grand event, which carried life-and-death consequences for them, by humbling themselves through physical self-denial (fasting, etc.) and keeping Sabbath by abstaining from work (Leviticus 16:29, 31; 23:26–32).[8] Thus they obeyed God and pledged allegiance to Him. By humbling themselves, they foreshadowed in small measure Christ's experience of faith: "He humbled Himself" (Philippians 2:8).

During the end-time Day of Atonement, which is the pre-Advent judgment, God wants His people to participate by doing two similar things: (1) by obeying His commandments, and (2) by hanging on to the faith of Jesus (Revelation 14:12). Revelation 14 says that when those who are saved reach safety on the other side of the crisis, they'll follow Christ wherever He leads them (verse 4). But they don't start following Him for the first time when they enter the pearly gates of the New Jerusalem. They'll follow Him in that place because that's what they have been accustomed to doing as they've been obeying God and holding on to Jesus' faith.

The basic call of the life of faith remains the same. Christians living at the end aren't required to have a unique quality of faith and loyalty that none of God's people have possessed in the past. It is true that Revelation 14:5 speaks of a special group of saved people who are "blameless." But thousands of years ago, God commanded Abraham, " 'Walk before Me, and be blameless' " (Genesis 17:1). The standard is the same, and there is no higher standard of harmony with God's will than that. Caleb loyally followed wherever the Lord led him. And so did Joseph, Daniel, Esther, John the Baptist, the apostles of Christ, and a host of others, who've obeyed God, trusted in His salvation, and accepted His guidance (see Hebrews 11). There is no higher level of following God's leadership than that.

"Walking" with God is the only way to become like Him in character—that is, to grow to maturity, to perfection. Enoch didn't gain the blessing of crossing over the threshold into the eternal world because he was sitting around trying to make himself perfect by gritting his teeth and pulling his faults out one by one. He gained it because he loved to be with his Lord. He gained strength and purity from accompanying his divine Master wherever He went. Enoch didn't have to make a great leap into Paradise; it was only a short step for him because he was already walking with God (Genesis 5:24). "When I think about becoming perfect in character, I start contemplating my faults and become afraid. Like Peter when he was walking on the water, I become distracted by obstacles—the wind and the waves—and I begin to sink (Matt 14:30). But when I think of being loyal to Christ, the picture changes because my gaze is on Him. He is my example, shepherd, and guardian (1 Pet 2:21-25). I gain courage because all I need to do is follow Him where He wants to take me, including to perfection of character. The result is similar—perfection of character—but the focus is different."[9]

We know the kind of faithfulness that God asks of us today. In the stories the Bible contains, we've seen it demonstrated in the lives of real people with faults, challenges, and weaknesses like ours. That's why it is so important that we study the whole Bible. By profiling the characteristics that God approves and those that He rejects and by letting us know that He's with us and helping us all the way, it teaches us how to act and speak and what attitudes we should strive to have.

Does the judgment place new requirements upon God's people? Revelation 14:12 specifies keeping God's commandments and holding fast to the faith of Jesus. These aren't new requirements, just as Jesus' " 'new commandment . . . that you love one another' " (John 13:34) was not new in itself (see Leviticus 19:18, 34); but was *renewed* for Christ's followers and given deeper meaning by His example. The book of Revelation renews and emphasizes the commands to obey God and keep Jesus' faith (including faith in Jesus) because these commands have special meaning for the people who live during the judgment, when the powers opposed to God challenge their obedience and faith. The quality of their loyalty will not be unique; they follow in the footsteps of people like Abraham and Caleb. But God will lead them through unique circumstances, which nobody has experienced before. Furthermore, in the end time, a whole group of people will unitedly cooperate with Him in this way.

Our culture tends to be highly individualistic, and each of us must have an individual relationship with Christ. However, His work in the world must be done by a unified community of believers who cooperate in using their varied spiritual gifts for reaching the lost with the love of God and the truth about His character. Christ's gospel commission to take the good news of salvation to the entire world before He comes (Matthew 24:14; 28:19, 20) will not be fulfilled through a few prima donnas who act as if they are the only ones who matter. Rather, it will be done through a divinely empowered, massive effort by many humble people working together as one, for whom the only thing that matters is glory to God through service to humankind. Yes, God, Your honor is what matters!

---

1. *The New Encyclopedia of Christian Quotations,* Mark Water, ed. (Grand Rapids: Baker, 2000), 1094.

2. On the identity and nature of the end-time "Babylon" in the book of Revelation, see *The Seventh-day Adventist Bible Commentary,* Francis D. Nichol, ed. (Hagerstown, Md.: Review and Herald, 1957) 7:828–830.

3. The remainder of the present chapter is adapted from Roy Gane, *Altar Call* (Berrien Springs, Mich.: Diadem, 1999), 314–343.

4. Amanda Ripley, "How to Get Out Alive," *Time* (May 2, 2005), 59.

5. Ibid.

6. Gane, 338.

7. John T. Anderson, *Investigating the Judgment* (Hagerstown, Md.: Review and Herald, 2003), 26.

8. For explanation of *self-denial,* see Roy Gane, *Leviticus, Numbers,* NIV Application Commentary (Grand Rapids: Zondervan, 2004), 404, 405; Roy Gane, *Cult and Character: Purification Offerings, Day of Atonement, and Theodicy* (Winona Lake, Ind.: Eisenbrauns, 2005), 312–315.

9. Gane, *Altar Call,* 333.

Conclusion: The Elijah Message and the Third Angel's Message

We have found that the third angel's message of Revelation 14:9–12 contains a two-fold message for the people who live during the judgment that takes place just before Jesus returns. It warns them against worshiping "the beast and its image," and it calls for "the endurance of the saints, those who keep the commandments of God and hold fast to the faith of Jesus" (verses 11, 12, NRSV).

At the very end of the Old Testament, Malachi recorded God's promise, " 'Behold, I am going to send you Elijah the prophet before the coming of the great and terrible day of the LORD. And he will restore the hearts of the fathers to their children, and the hearts of the children to their fathers, lest I come and smite the land with a curse' " (Malachi 4:5, 6). The Elijah figure does his work of reconciling families before "the great and terrible day of the LORD," which must be Christ's second coming (see Revelation 6:15–17; 14:14–20; 19:11–21). This at least overlaps with the time of the pre-Advent judgment, when the third angel's message is proclaimed. What then is the relationship between the Elijah message of Malachi and the third angel's message of Revelation?

The Elijah message implies judgment. Before God holds people accountable for the ways they have related to each other, He gives them an opportunity to be reconciled to one another, especially within families and across generations. The prophecy that the Elijah message will "restore the hearts" of people to each other indicates that it will involve a renewal of love for each other.

Conclusion: The Elijah Message and the Third Angel's Message

The third angel's message also calls for love: God's commandments are based on love for God and our fellow human beings (see Matthew 22:37–40). And its call that people "hold fast to the faith of Jesus" exhorts people to maintain trust like that which Christ had in His Father's will to save us through His loving sacrifice and to have faith in Jesus to deliver us because He loves us so much that He died for us. Because of the love Jesus has shown for us, He has commanded us that we " 'love one another, even as I have loved you, that you also love one another' " (John 13:34).

So, the third angel's message embraces the Elijah message. Their thrust is the same, except that the Elijah message more narrowly emphasizes relational reconciliation between parents and children. Those who do not accept the Elijah message are cursed (Malachi 4:6), and those who reject the third angel's message, choosing the unloving "beast and his image" rather than the loving God, suffer destruction by fire and brimstone (Revelation 14:10). This shows that love for one another is essential for our survival. Those who live with God, His holy angels, and redeemed human beings for all eternity in the next life will be those whose hearts have been loving toward others in the present age that is passing away.

In the parable of the sheep and the goats (Matthew 25:31–46), Jesus said the verdict of the pre-Advent judgment would be based on the way we treat those in need—which, He said, reveals how we would have treated Him when He was here on earth. The examples of situations that Jesus gives are breathtakingly simple, practical, and doable: " ' "I was hungry, and you gave Me something to eat; I was thirsty, and you gave Me drink; I was a stranger, and you invited Me in; naked, and you clothed Me; I was sick, and you visited Me; I was in prison, and you came to Me" ' " (verses 35, 36). Everyone can do these kinds of things. They don't require an eighth grade certificate, let alone a college diploma or a master of divinity degree.

Of course, Jesus didn't intend to limit what He expects us to do for each other to the small list that He mentioned in this parable. His point was that we are to help others in need, whether they are family members, friends, or strangers. A woman may need a hug to reassure her that her hard work and care for her family is appreciated. A man may need help washing dishes and doing laundry as he tries to keep the household going while his wife is studying toward a degree. A son may need help with his math, and a teenage daughter may need to talk about relationships at school. A single person may need some encouragement and a prayer. An elderly person may need a ride to buy groceries. A friend may be in difficulty regarding a job or because of financial or marital distress. A stranger may need directions or help changing a tire by the side of the highway. The possibilities go on and on. The common factor is love for others.

Mother Teresa said, "Jesus comes to meet us. To welcome Him, let us go to meet Him. He comes to us in the hungry, the naked, the lonely, the alcoholic, the drug addict, the prostitute, the street beggars. He may come to you or me in a father who is alone, in a mother, in a brother, or in a sister. If we reject them, if we do not go out to meet them, we reject Jesus himself."[1]

We can't meet the needs of everyone. Even Jesus Himself could be in only one place at a time, so He had to be selective. But He did seek out those who were in deep needs of various kinds, and He didn't ignore an urgent, genuine plea for help.

Of course, we know there are con artists who prey on modern Christians to extort help that they do not really need. The apostle Paul taught that we have no obligation to provide for those who are able to work but are "motivationally challenged"—politically correct for "lazy." If they go hungry, that is entirely up to them. Paul said, "If anyone will not work, neither let him eat" (2 Thessalonians 3:10). These are not the people Jesus was talking about in Matthew 25. There He asks us to help those with real needs.

Malachi and John's third angel call us to repent of our uncooperative unlove that fragments our unity and thereby dilutes our witness for Christ in the world. There is one God, one Savior, one faith, one baptism, and one church body of fellowship (see Ephesians 4:4–6). It is time to return to the Messiah who has brought us together, to put aside our differences, to revel in our God-given diversity, to pull toward the banner of the uplifted Christ (see John 12:32) at the center of our faith, and to march victoriously through the end of the great war to the great peace on the other side!

---

1. *Mother Teresa: In My Own Words,* José Luis González-Balado, compiler (New York: Gramercy Books, 1996), 29.